MY STORY, MY SONG

MY STORY, MY SONG

MOTHER-DAUGHTER REFLECTIONS ON LIFE AND FAITH

Lucimarian Roberts
as told to Missy Buchanan

with reflections by

ROBIN ROBERTS

UPPER ROOM BOOKS®
NASHVILLE

My Story, My Song
Mother-Daughter Reflections on Life and Faith
Copyright © 2012 by Lucimarian Roberts
All rights reserved.

Upper Room®, Upper Room Books®, and design logos are trademarks owned by The Upper Room®, a Ministry of GBOD®, Nashville, Tennessee. All rights reserved.
The Upper Room Web site: http:/www.upperroom.org

Scripture quotations are taken from THE HOLY BIBLE, NEW INTERNATIONAL VERSION®, NIV® Copyright © 1973, 1978, 1984, 2011 by Biblica, Inc.,™ Used by permission. All rights reserved worldwide.

"Prayer for Protection" by James Dillet Freeman used with permission of Unity, www.unity.org.
Some text on page 76 is adapted from Robin Roberts, *From the Heart: Eight Rules to Live By* (Hyperion, 2008, Kindle edition).

Cover Photo: Glade Bilby II
Cover and Interior Design: Marc Whitaker, mtwdesign.net
Typesetting: PerfecType, Nashville, TN

LIBRARY OF CONGRESS CATALOGING IN PUBLICATION
Roberts, Lucimarian.
  My story, my song : mother-daughter reflections on life and faith / by Lucimarian Roberts ; as told to Missy Buchanan ; reflections by Robin Roberts.
      p. cm.
  ISBN 978-0-8358-1107-1 — ISBN 978-0-8358-1108-8 (eBook)
1. Mothers—Religious life. 2. Daughters—Religious life.
3. Christian women—Religious life. 4. Mothers and daughters—Religious aspects—Christianity. 5. Roberts, Lucimarian. 6. Roberts, Robin
I. Buchanan, Missy. II. Roberts, Robin III. Title.
  BV4529.18.R59 2011
  248.8'431—dc23   2011053109

Printed in the United States of America

This book is dedicated to God, who has loved,

guided, and protected me all my life.

And to the four children God gave me

to love, guide, and protect:

a handsome son, Lawrence (Butch),

and three beautiful daughters,

Sally-Ann, Dorothy, and Robin,

who now love, guide, and protect me.

Praise God from whom all blessings flow!

Contents

Foreword

I so wish the wisdom Lucimarian Roberts shares in *My Story, My Song: Mother-Daughter Reflections on Life and Faith* could have been placed in my hands and heart earlier. Surely it would have made the everyday of my life easier. It would have opened the way to conscious change and order, harmony, clarity, and love when I was wildly seeking in the wrong places for what is ever so near. Miss Lucimarian's wisdom would have accelerated my spiritual growth as well as lessened my self-doubt and heartache.

Not that my own mother didn't share her wisdom with me. Babs never let up or let me go. But the mother-daughter dyad causes emotions to run high. When mothers speak truths we'd rather not hear, children look the other way. Most of what my Babs cautioned and counseled when I was a girl—and a young woman even—fell on deaf ears. Now that she's gone, I quote my beloved mother every day.

An intimate meditation, *My Story, My Song* is a book to treasure, to read in the quiet, to let seep in, and to share with others to help them along their journey.

Robin's reflections go straight to the heart. They gave me insight into the Roberts family. The family members I have met seem so at home with themselves. Their smiles, hugs, and warm, welcoming words greet you and draw you

near. Their peace is evident; it invites you in. You sense it in
Robin. Her sincerity and joy, her intelligence—always asking the right questions—that sharp mind and kind heart at
work. This is why we tune in to *Good Morning America*—
surely to get the morning news but also for that morning
dose of get-up-and-go, that can-do spirit we so need each
day to step out on the good foot in this challenging, trou-
bled world. These reflections provide a peek into Robin's
background. Her moral intelligence and exhilaration in
being alive, the authenticity that compelled her to share
her fight against breast cancer with the world—such courage and walk-on-water faith were planted by her mother.

I know best Robin's big sis, Sally-Ann—a burst of light
and one of the most tender and compassionate souls I've ever
met. She is named for Lucimarian's mother, about whom
Lucimarian writes passionately and powerfully. The senior
Sally, Lucimarian tells us, lived, loved, and worked fiercely
to protect her children during some of the cruelest times for
African Americans in this nation.

Like Lucimarian, Robin and her sister Sally-Ann know
deep love as something natural, not something alien we must
learn to do but innate in the God in all of us. Life on earth
today and what we allow make it evident that we have loving
to do. I see now how the Roberts sisters came to know that
heaven is here on earth and that only love is real. It is through
the wisdom and grace of Mother Lucimarian Roberts.

Black women, all women, must tell our stories. Speaking our truth connects us with the power of courage. Having our say transforms our fears into trust. Our cries open up portals and doorways, spiritual pathways to healing. We see that everything in our lives is teaching us about ourselves. Poet and writer Audre Lorde put it this way: "I have come to believe over and over again that what is most important to me must be spoken, made verbal and shared, even at the risk of having it bruised or misunderstood."

My Story, My Song documents the spirit and strength of black women; how without hesitation or apology, black women resist the forces that would oppress us and undermine our inner authority. In the final analysis we learned from our mothers, as they did from theirs, to trust the end to God. Lucimarian's story brings from the fringes an inspiring history grounded in the complexities and challenges women face in navigating the pathways home to ourselves—while struggling to make love work, keep peace in our family, earn a living, stay strong in body and soul, stave off the doubts and fears forever nipping at our heels.

In Lucimarian's intimate writings we see that having faith and connecting with our purpose combine to bring us peace. We witness how so elegant and beautiful a woman lived through "the ugly years of segregation." How the disrespect shown her when racism reared its head didn't take root in her as bitterness. How she withstood disappointment and constant relocation that might have unraveled her fifty-seven-years-strong marriage. We see grace and a capacity to love in full force as Lucimarian recounts packing up all their belongings and reestablishing the family home some twenty-seven times for her beloved husband, Larry, a Tuskegee Airman whose military career kept them constantly on the move.

Lucimarian Roberts is a gifted musician, and making music has quieted her mind and deepened her insight. Still does. Playing the piano and singing spirituals passed down through the generations bring her peace. The resonance and rhythms, the words of praise and affirmation soothe her. All of her life she has been a singer, and so she turns to what is sure. Her music is her joy and how she praises God! Her music is her comfort when she is sad, feeling lonely or lost, or seeking guidance or confirmation. Her music is meditation, a space in which she communes with the Holy Spirit. Making time for inner stillness, listening in, is the key to self-discovery and the peace and surety we're all seeking.

This is what we glean from *My Story, My Song*, from Lucimarian and Robin Roberts: With faith and our hearts filled with gratitude, we drink from the well that never runs dry.

—Susan L. Taylor
Founder, National CARES Mentoring Movement
Editor-in-Chief Emerita, *Essence* magazine

Introduction

The mother-daughter relationship is one of life's glorious mysteries. Can I get an *Amen?* It can run the gamut of emotions; I'll let you fill in the blank yourself.

I'm grateful to God for blessing my mom with many years on this earth. It has given our relationship a chance to evolve and grow—from shouting matches that ended with Mom saying, "Why? Because I'm the Momma and I said so, that's why!" to seeing her not just as my mom but also as a true, dear friend. (I'm still trying to figure out how that happened.)

Good Morning America viewers grieved with me when my beloved father died in 2004. They marveled at my mother's strength and grace after his passing. Stories that include my family have been well received by the *GMA* audience. Folks are drawn to Mom's humility, wisdom, and spirituality. I've been told countless times: "Your mother should write a book." Well, just as the beautiful hymn that I have been blessed to hear Mom sing, says, . . . *This is her story.*

—Robin Roberts

SINGING BECAUSE I MUST

On most days, I slide onto the piano bench just as the evening shadows fall across the living room of my Mississippi home. It is my refuge. It is where I come to meet with God.

There are songbooks and hymnals stacked in a basket in the corner of the room. Usually, though, my fingers just take to the keys without conscious thought. Most often it is an old hymn that takes flight—like a prayer with a melody reaching far back into my childhood.

I know that God is always with me, but there's something special about having a particular place to meet together. As I look around the familiar room, I am reminded of both the joy and the heartache that have dwelled within these walls. This is the welcoming place that our family called home after living in twenty-six other places while my husband, Larry, served as an officer in the U.S. Air Force. It is where I came to help heal my broken heart after Larry died at age eighty-one.

This is the place where laughter and music have filled the rooms during holiday gatherings with family and friends. It is also where the floodwaters of Hurricane Katrina swallowed up the entire first floor, destroying every memento and home furnishing in its muddy grasp.

Today in the solitude of this refurbished room, I play the piano and sing.

I sing words of songs I memorized as a child growing up in the 1920s and 1930s in Akron, Ohio. I sing tunes I learned at school and in my grandparents' home whenever the family would gather around the piano for a sing-along. I sing the spirituals and songs I first heard in the small Church of God where my grandfather was a lay pastor.

I sing because the music of the church speaks my soul language. I sing because these songs are tightly woven into the texture of who I am. Lucimarian Tolliver Roberts. Child of God.

Actually, I was a grown woman before I discovered that my mother had not intended to name me Lucimarian. She had chosen the name of Moses' sister, Miriam, for the second half of my name. Somehow though, *Lucimiriam* became *Lucimarian*. My mother had no recollection of how it got changed, and I suppose it really doesn't matter since I've been Lucimarian for as long as I can remember.

BORN TO MAKE MUSIC

When I was growing up in Akron, my maternal grandparents lived down the street in what we kids fondly referred to as The House. My grandparents, George and Lizzy Suddeth, encouraged me to play the old player piano in their small living room whenever I visited. Somehow I was able to hear a song, then sit down at the piano and replicate it in my own style. Some might say it was a gift, unexplained except by the grace of God. However, I don't think my piano teachers would have agreed that it was a gift at all!

Times were hard and money was scarce, but my resourceful mother found a way to pay for piano lessons. I remember eyeing the first teacher's long, bony fingers and sensing her stern disposition, a precursor of her teaching style. She seemed to delight in having me repeat scale exercises while constantly correcting my fingering patterns. After just a few weeks, she informed my mother that she was wasting her time since I already had formed terrible piano techniques.

Not long after, a second piano teacher came to the same conclusion. She was a talented musician, firmly entrenched in classical music, especially the compositions of Bach, Beethoven, and Haydn. But my mother noticed that my joy was draining away under the teacher's instruction. Though she never dismissed the value of lessons and persistence, my mother recognized that formal piano training wasn't a good match for my play-by-ear style. Once the lessons ceased, my joy returned.

In many ways, singing the music of the church came as naturally to me as breathing. Perhaps it was because of people like Frank and Norman Terry who worked with the music program at our little church and introduced me to the deep expressions of spirituals and well-loved hymns. The Terry brothers had moved to Ohio after attending the Piney Woods School, a historic school for black children in impoverished, rural Mississippi. The school's academic and spiritual influence on the Terry brothers was profound. These two highly creative men had a passion for learning sparked by their days at Piney Woods. They were eager to broaden the musical horizons of our congregation by teaching us hymns and songs they had learned as boys. I loved the haunting melodies and moving lyrics of songs like "Deep River" and "There Is a Balm in Gilead."

When I was in the seventh grade, Norman Terry selected three girls to form a trio. Evelyn Wilson, Dorothy Marcus, and I rehearsed on Sunday afternoons at my home where I would thump out the accompaniment on an old upright piano given to us by a family who employed my mother as a domestic worker. Mr. Terry directed us and made suggestions as we rehearsed. Our trio often sang during the

Sunday-school hour at church, but we were not allowed to sing at the eleven o'clock service since we had not yet made a profession of faith. People said our voices blended beautifully, and soon we began to receive invitations to sing at other churches and events around the community. Every time we had the opportunity to sing together, I thanked God for giving me the gift of music. Our trio sang together until I left for college six years later.

Just a few years ago, one of the trio members, Evelyn, spoke at a choir reunion hosted by our childhood church. As an eighty-something-year-old woman, she was delighted that the worship service included many of the old hymns and spirituals our trio had sung so long ago, including one of my favorites, "Spirit Holy." Evelyn had never moved from Akron and had been a church member since the day she had run past Dorothy and me to get to the altar and dedicate herself to Christ. She was a teenager at the time. Now as one of the oldest members and a former choir member, she was asked to share her thoughts with the congregation.

Evelyn talked about how much it meant to her to have known all the words to the songs they sang that day. She encouraged congregants to hold firm to their faith and not get distracted by the worldly things of this life. Then she took a step down, collapsed, and died in front of the church! Since that morning, I have often thought about how Evelyn left this world with a glorious testimony on her lips.

Spirit Holy

Spirit holy, Spirit holy,
All my being now possess;
Lead me, rule me, work within me,
Through my life Thy will express.

Another church member with a passion for music and drama had a tremendous influence on me as a young person. Hattie Rice directed the children and youth pageants at my church, elaborate productions, especially for their day. For years Miss Rice had been a seamstress, but on her own time, she was a theatrical wizard. She was not only the director and scriptwriter but also the lighting specialist and stage manager. Every year she wrote a fresh script and created new staging and scenery. We kids didn't even mind that she was a strict disciplinarian who expected us to know our lines, stand up straight, and project our voices.

On Christmas Eve the lights of the church would dim, making the potbelly stove glow red-hot in the darkness. The wooden church overflowed with people eager to watch the nativity story come alive in music and drama. One memorable year Miss Rice rigged a pulley for the star of the East, creating a spectacular scene that caused people to gasp. Each year we would also celebrate the resurrection of Christ with an equally elaborate Easter pageant just a few months later.

It might seem odd that childhood pageants have left such an imprint on me at this late stage of life. Though I can't fully explain it, those special events did impact my spiritual journey. Even now I recall how privileged I felt to participate in a sacred celebration of Christ's life.

———•◦•———

My years at Robinson Elementary School in Akron also hold wonderful memories. When one teacher taught us to sing songs in rounds, it seemed like magic. Another teacher introduced me to four-part harmony, then to operas like *Aida* and *Madama Butterfly*. Year by year, it seemed I received more opportunities to sing in choirs and ensembles, culminating in the honor of singing a solo at my own high school graduation.

Music played an important role during my time as a student at Howard University too. I sang in the chapel choir, and each year I participated in a singing competition hosted by the dormitories on campus. Fortunately, I won the competition for several years in a row. Perhaps that was when I began to understand that my musical abilities brought me respect from my peers, who were often more wealthy and worldly than I.

Hymns of Comfort and Strength

Music got me through the loneliest time of my life when I was a young wife and mother. My husband, Larry, was assigned to a U.S. Air Force base in Japan, so we left behind family and friends and moved across the Pacific Ocean with our firstborn, Butch, who was just a toddler. For the first four months we lived in a few tiny rooms in a Quonset hut. But nothing prepared me for the isolation I'd feel as the only black woman on base in a foreign country. On days when the loneliness became almost unbearable, I would go to the base chapel, which was open twenty-four hours a day. I'd slip inside the empty chapel, go straight to the piano, and begin to play hymns and sing. By the time I left an hour or so later, I felt revived. I have often wondered what I would have done without the hymns and scripture to comfort me then and countless other times.

Years later, in November of 2004, I was still reeling in grief from Larry's unexpected death. He had passed away in his sleep just a month earlier. Though our family usually gathered at our home in Pass Christian, Mississippi, for Thanksgiving, I wasn't up for hosting it that year. I decided to change tradition and go to New York to celebrate quietly with my daughter Robin. When Robin's friend Diane Sawyer discovered that we would be in the city for the holiday, she insisted that Robin and I share the Thanksgiving meal with her and an eclectic group of family and friends.

Diane's gracious spirit shone throughout her lovely apartment that autumn day. But I must admit that I was more than a little surprised when actress Candice Bergen suddenly appeared with a tray of appetizers. All I could think was *Murphy Brown is serving me hors d'oeuvres!* And for the first time, I learned that Diane's husband, Mike Nichols, was a famous film and stage director. I had always just known him as Mike.

After hors d'oeuvres, we made our way to Ms. Bergen's nearby apartment where we sat around a large dining table for the main course. Each of us was asked to make a comment or share a reflection. When my turn came, I began to sing an old spiritual I had known since childhood—"We'll Understand It Better By and By." Just as I got to the chorus, another voice joined me. I looked around to see that it was Diane, singing the harmony line. Though she never mentioned it, I later learned that she had once been a member of the Blue Notes, an *a cappella* group at Wellesley College. After dinner, Carly Simon and her son, Ben, sang a beautiful song to conclude the celebration.

I will long remember that Thanksgiving gathering as a sweet moment in time. Music embraced my grief and helped me to celebrate life once again.

We'll Understand It Better By and By

By and by, when the morning comes,
when the saints of God are gathered home,
we'll tell the story how we've overcome,
for we'll understand it better by and by.

In August 2005, Hurricane Katrina swept across the Mississippi Gulf Coast with its powerful wind and storm surge. I had decided to ride out the hurricane at my Biloxi home since I was experiencing excruciating back pain and didn't think I could travel. My daughter Dorothy and her two daughters refused to evacuate without me, so they came to stay with me instead. None of us knew just how monstrous Katrina was until the full force of the rains came and the winds began to howl. It was unlike anything I'd experienced in other hurricanes. Tree limbs broke like matchsticks and flew through the air. Part of the roof blew off, leaving the home's interior exposed to the rain. With no power or telephone service, we were cut off from the world, but inwardly I knew we were not cut off from God. And so I did what I always do when I find myself in uncertain circumstances. I went to the piano and began to sing hymns.

In 2011 I spent several hours in a recording studio taping some of my favorite hymns and spirituals. Dorothy contributed her beautiful soprano voice since my voice is not as high and strong as it once was. The studio time was a gift from my daughter Robin, but the CD recording is my gift to my family. Over the last few years, I have come to realize how much I want my grandchildren and great-grandchildren to be familiar with the songs of my childhood. I hope they will internalize the lyrics and the melodies that helped get me through difficult days throughout my life. Now that I'm in my late eighties, I want them to know the hymns that still bring me comfort as I face increasing physical limitations and the losses that come with aging.

Some are simple songs, like "Jesus Loves Me." Others, like "It Is Well with My Soul," speak to the hardships that are sure to come along life's journey.

It Is Well with My Soul

When peace, like a river, attendeth my way,
when sorrows like sea billows roll;
> *whatever my lot, thou hast taught me to say,*
> *It is well, it is well with my soul.*
Though Satan should buffet, though trials should come,
let this blest assurance control,
> *that Christ has regarded my helpless estate,*
> *and hath shed his own blood for my soul.*
> *It is well, it is well with my soul.*

As I look across my long life, I realize that the music of the church has been my saving grace. It has stirred my soul and brought me great comfort. Even as my journey continues, I am certain that the sound of these songs will carry me through to the very end.

PSALM 28:6-8

Praise be to the LORD,
for he has heard my cry for mercy.
The LORD is my strength and my shield;
my heart trusts in him, and he helps me.
My heart leaps for joy,
and with my song I praise him.
The LORD is the strength of his people,
a fortress of salvation for his anointed one.

Robin's *Reflection*

The first Thanksgiving after Daddy died was so hard. Mom came up to be with me in New York because being at home would have been too painful. My dear friend and colleague Diane Sawyer, who attended my father's funeral in Mississippi, insisted we join her for the holiday. We had appetizers at Diane's home and dinner at Candice Bergen's. (I was so worried Mom was going to call her Murphy Brown!)

I'll never forget Mom leaning over to me after the blessing to whisper: "How can you have Thanksgiving dinner without mashed potatoes?"

I think it was the first time I had heard Momma laugh since Daddy died weeks earlier.

The most beautiful sight for me is seeing Mom at the piano. I can hear her sweet voice right now. In fact, I don't remember a time when music did not fill our home. Mom made me and my siblings take piano lessons until a certain age. Then we could decide whether or not to continue with the lessons. As soon as it became optional, I bolted for the front door—no more piano lessons for me. It's one of the few regrets I have in life, especially when I see how much comfort playing the piano and singing have brought into Mom's life.

Chapter 2

KNOWING THAT HOME IS WHEREVER WE ARE

I remember the day that strangers came to repossess my parents' beautiful bedroom furniture. It was a lovely, dusty-rose set with graceful green leaves; it included a vanity and stool, a headboard and footboard, and a large chest of drawers. The year was 1929, and I was just five years old.

A queasy feeling came over me as I watched men awkwardly march into our home like uninvited guests. When I glanced at my mother's face, I knew something was terribly wrong. Even from across the room I could see tears trickling down her cheeks. Perhaps that is why I was surprised when she graciously instructed the men on how best to carry the furniture down the stairs and turn each piece a certain way as they came to the landing so that the dusty-rose paint wouldn't get scratched.

In a few days the men returned to take our living room sofas. Not long after that, I began to notice other things disappearing too. The crystal doorknobs. The patterned rugs. The wall tapestry. I don't know for sure, but I assume that my mother quietly sold the items as an additional source of income.

Soon after the bedroom furniture was removed, my mother took a job as a domestic worker, earning a dollar a day. I didn't fully understand it at the time, but I later realized how humbling it must have been for her to have had her most prized possessions paraded out the door by a band of strangers, then have to get a job cleaning houses for well-to-do families. When people asked her why she was working outside the home, she simply answered that she had to pay the mortgage. Still, I never heard my mother complain. She had the most marvelous way of taking what life served her and making the best of it. Those days were a stressful transition for our entire family. For as long as I could remember, my mother, Sally Tolliver, had been at home, caring for my older brother, William, my younger sister, Depholia, and me.

Creating a Loving Home in Unstable Times

Looking back to those childhood days, I recognize my mother's remarkable dedication to creating a loving, stable home in spite of unstable circumstances. For most of my youth, my father's presence was unpredictable. He came and went, depending on his sobriety, but my mother's commitment to family and to her Christian faith remained strong. We were in church every Sunday, and she taught us that success in life is never about money. It is about integrity and character. She often told us kids, "You may be poor, but you don't have to be common." That simple but profound statement has stayed with me.

In the early years of my parents' marriage, my father had successfully created small business ventures that allowed our family to live comfortably. Even so, his success did not come without controversy. When I was an infant, my father operated a poolroom in a rented space near the Akron apartment where our family first lived. My grandfather, a strict Church of God lay pastor, forcefully objected to his son-in-law's business endeavor, believing it promoted gambling and drinking. And in fact, over the span of my childhood, my father's relationship with my mother's father was often tenuous.

My father, William (Bill) Tolliver, was originally from West Virginia but had moved to Lake Erie in 1918 to take a job as a cook before becoming a bellhop at the Portage Hotel in Akron where my mother worked as an elevator operator. A year or so after they met, they married on their lunch hour at the courthouse. There was no minister, no family members, no church wedding. My grandparents were devastated.

It could be that my grandfather was also upset because my mother's paycheck would no longer go to him, as had been the custom since she had first gone to work.

My grandparents had hoped that my mother would wed one of the two young attorneys from the neighborhood who were pursuing her. But I think she had already been smitten with my father's great sense of humor, his worldliness, and his good looks.

A few years later, my father developed a business in which he provided parking, auto repair, and car washes to the Goodyear executives who had offices adjacent to his garage. His business was so successful that my parents bought a sedan convertible and a brand-new house just up the street from my grandparents. Not long after, my father sold the business to Goodyear; and they hired him back as the manager of the garage. But when the stock market tumbled in 1929, marking the start of the Great Depression, our comfortable lifestyle vanished. In many ways, my father vanished also. He began to drink quite heavily. It wasn't long before he lost his job at Goodyear. There were countless times when he would disappear for two or three days at a stretch, leaving my mother to make a living and hold the family together.

Just after the furniture was repossessed, the electricity and gas in our home were turned off because the bills had gone unpaid. My father had spent the money on a three-day drinking binge. I will never forget how my mother's voice choked with disappointment and anger as she confronted him. "How could you do this to us?" she kept repeating. I watched my father bury his face in his hands and begin to weep. It was a pitiful scene—the only time I remember seeing my father cry.

Even the water in our house dwindled down to a trickle. My mother, who had grown accustomed to cooking on a four-burner gas stove, was now forced to use a wood-burning stove that my uncle had rigged in the basement so that the smoke could be released through the flue. As a young child, I remember being terribly embarrassed to see smoke curling from our chimney on a hot August day.

Embarrassment struck again when my mother posted a sign in the front window for the ice man who delivered blocks of ice for refrigeration. The blocks came in different sizes: twenty-five, fifty, and one hundred pounds. Almost always, my mother marked the box for a twenty-five-pound block—a glaring sign, it seemed, that we could afford only the bare minimum.

My father had a number of friends who were politicians, and he often worked in their campaigns. As long as he was sober, he displayed a gregarious personality and keen business skills. If the politician won his election, he would help find my father a more permanent job. Sometimes the jobs lasted for a while, but usually my father's drinking problem caused him to be fired within a short time.

One time my brother and I went riding with my father in a bakery delivery truck. He'd gotten a job driving the white commercial van with the help of a political friend. We were speeding down a big hill with a traffic light at the bottom. My brother and I knew that our father had been drinking. We looked at each other, eyes wide, watching loaves of bread, donuts, and sweet rolls wildly bounce up and down on the racks, some falling to the floor. Mostly we were worried that the traffic light at the bottom of the hill would turn red and our father would drive through the intersection, perhaps killing all of us. Thankfully, the light turned green just in time.

Instead of the store-bought clothes we had once worn, my siblings and I began to wear hand-me-down clothes that my mother received from the families for whom she worked. Later I learned that she often chose jobs based on the ages of the children in the family, praying that their clothes might be passed down to us.

If my mother had a touch of regret for having married my father, she never revealed it in front of us children. Though he had only a sixth-grade education, my father was bright with entrepreneurial ideas. But sadly, his drinking proved devastating to our family. Eventually my mother had to take on a second job to pay the bills. After a full day of cleaning houses, she went to work at a teahouse in the evenings. For my siblings and me, there was an upside to her job at the teahouse though. Occasionally she brought us leftover treats, including miniature pears, which we adored.

On days when we had little food in the house, my mother would spread a blanket and create a picnic under the apple tree in the backyard. Most often the picnic featured a can of Vienna sausages or a tin of sardines and crackers, which we washed down with Kool-Aid. If we were lucky, there would be a single hard-boiled egg sliced into four pieces, one for each of us kids and one for my mother. Instead of grumbling about how poor we really were, she turned the situation into an *alfresco* dining adventure.

Indeed my mother had a special knack for transforming the mundane into something fun. I recall the little smile on her lips when she first gave us children pieces of chalk and invited us to draw on the wallpaper in the sunroom. Ordinarily, such behavior would have been forbidden, but she allowed us this childhood fantasy. We would draw for hours and then use an old rag to wipe the wallpaper clean.

Each afternoon after school, my brother, sister, and I would go to The House, my grandparents' home down the street, and stay until my mother could pick us up. Though she must have been bone-tired, she would challenge us children to a footrace home. She would give us a big head start, then pass us like a deer, using her long stride and great athleticism to beat us every time.

On many raw winter days, I would burst into a frigid house because there had been no money to buy coal. My mother would check on us during the night to make sure that we were warm enough under a pile of blankets. She also made sure we had a newspaper in our home. Although she had no formal education beyond the sixth grade, she was both intelligent and wise. Reading the newspaper was her way of showing us how she valued education and keeping up with the events of the day.

My mother kept a scrapbook full of news stories about African-American role models. One story recounted how renowned singer and activist Marian Anderson sang before 75,000 people at the Lincoln Memorial after the Daughters of the American Revolution refused to allow her to sing at their Constitution Hall. Other clippings described black writers involved in the Harlem Renaissance and the Fisk University Jubilee Singers, a black ensemble who sang old spirituals and traveled the world in an effort to break down racial barriers. When the Jubilee Singers came to Akron, my mother's friend took me to their performance. That scrapbook signified how much my mother wanted to inspire us. She wanted us to understand that with hard work, perseverance, and integrity, black children could grow up to achieve their dreams like anyone else.

My mother insisted on having a tidy home. She believed that people tend to judge others by what they see on the exterior of your house, regardless of its size. If they see a home in disarray, they assume that the people who live inside are probably uncaring or unmotivated too. Even when times were hard, my mother kept our home neatly manicured. The yard overflowed with lovely plants—honeysuckle on a trellis and lots of colorful primrose. Being the frugal person she was, she would root cuttings given to her from neighbors and friends, and then carefully tend them to maturity.

MAKING A HOME IN TWENTY-SEVEN DIFFERENT PLACES

After Larry and I married and had four children of our own, I came to realize how much my mother's perspective had influenced my own life. Each of our children was born in a different state, attesting to the truth that life as a military family is in a constant state of motion. Lawrence Jr., "Butch," was born in Ohio, Sally-Ann in Arizona. Dorothy was born in Iowa, and Robin in Alabama, each four years apart. It was vitally important to me to make each of the twenty-seven places we lived a home. As soon as we arrived at a housing assignment, I would immediately unpack the boxes and get things in order so that the children would be surrounded with familiar things and feel the stability of home. Larry and I would always remind them, "Home is wherever we are."

Each evening our family ate dinner by candlelight. In reality, I confess I had an ulterior motive. I wanted to artfully disguise the awful shade of paint that was typical in military housing. But for our family, candlelight at dinner signaled something much more important. It meant that we were together, and this was home. Let's give thanks to God and celebrate.

When we were living in Tuskegee, Alabama, I'd set up a picnic table on the screened-in front porch of our home so we could dine outside when the weather was nice. I lit the hurricane lamps just as a fashionably dressed woman passed by on her way home from the nearby veterinary school. I had often seen her and sometimes felt a twinge of jealousy, imagining what it would be like to be such a refined professional woman. Later, when she and I actually met, I discovered that this woman had walked by our home on many evenings, admiring our family gathering and the glowing hurricane lamps. I think we had each been swayed by envy.

I enjoyed making family mealtimes feel special. During those times when I taught school, I would set the breakfast table the night before so that it would be ready to welcome family members the next morning. I tried to accommodate each of the children's breakfast preferences. Butch liked eggs, over easy. Sally-Ann preferred French toast or pancakes since she didn't care for eggs. Dorothy was happy with a bowl of Raisin Bran, and Robin usually asked for a bacon-egg sandwich. My mother often called me a short-order cook, but I took pleasure in giving my children a positive experience to start their day.

BUILDING LIVES OF FAITH AND LOVE

Over the years I collected many china dish patterns and interesting silver and copper serving pieces to make the dinner table feel special. Now I sometimes worry that I spent too much time polishing and scrubbing instead of coloring or playing games with the children. Even so, I feel confident that my children knew that home was a place where we came together to build lives of faith and love.

I credit my mother for first creating that kind of home for me. She was only seventeen years old when she moved with her parents to Akron from Jacksons' Gap, Alabama, where my grandfather had been a sharecropper. She lived through the Depression and held her own family together through sheer ingenuity and hard work. Her life was not easy, yet she did not whine. Sally Tolliver was almost ninety-one years old when she died, an amazing role model and a woman of deep faith.

Reflecting on her life reminds me of two questions she frequently asked us children: "When you lie down at night, can you close your eyes knowing that you have been within the will of God today?" And then, "When you leave this world, will you be able to honestly say that you have done the best you could do?" I take those questions seriously. Each evening I think about my answers, knowing that even on those days when I have fallen short, God's grace will carry me through.

Jesus Loves Me

Jesus loves me! This I know, for the Bible tells me so.
Little ones to him belong; they are weak, but he is strong.
Yes, Jesus loves me! Yes, Jesus loves me!
Yes, Jesus loves me! The Bible tells me so.

DEUTERONOMY 6:4-9

Hear, O Israel: The LORD our God,
the LORD is one. Love the LORD your God
with all your heart and with all your soul and with all
your strength. These commandments that I give you
today are to be on your hearts. Impress them on your
children. Talk about them when you sit at home and
when you walk along the road, when you lie down and
when you get up. Tie them as symbols on your hands
and bind them on your foreheads. Write them on the
doorframes of your houses and on your gates.

Robin's *Reflection*

Elegant is the word most often used to describe Mom. Sometimes it's easy to forget her humble beginnings, but she hasn't forgotten. Grandma Sally may not have had much of a formal education, but she instilled values in Mom that remain with her today. Mom made our stark military housing a warm home. We ate dinner by candlelight even if we were eating franks and beans!

I didn't realize it then, but Mom had her own dreams that she sacrificed for her family. Grandma Sally wanted a better life for Mom, and Mom wanted that for her children.

When I was young and about to leave the house to hang with my friends, Mom would say to me, "You know the difference between right and wrong." Thanks to Mom I did—and still do.

Chapter 3

LEARNING THAT IT'S NOT ALL BLACK AND WHITE

For much of my life, I have had to deal with people who thought I was too black to be white and too white to be black. It has always seemed a strange phenomenon to me, since I am the same person inside. There have been times when white people shunned me without ever getting to know me. They just saw the color of my skin and turned away. But there have also been times when black people shook their heads as soon as they discovered that I had white friends. They thought I had somehow betrayed my ethnic heritage.

It seems I often had a foot in two different worlds. One black. One white. The two worlds were very different yet also alike. Even as a youngster, I wondered why skin color should make a difference in how we treat one another.

Throughout my life, I have tried to live my mother's mantra: Do not take on another's hatred. What wonderful wisdom! Like her, I have found that the best way to change a person's prejudice is to model a Christlike life. Only then are we able to rise above bitterness, anger, and revenge. After all, God is the Creator of us all, no matter the color of our skin.

RACISM IN THE EARLY YEARS

I was born in 1924, so I lived through the ugly years of segregation. Yet as a child, I was protected from the worst racial discrimination. Certainly Akron was not free of people with a racist mentality, but our neighborhood in the Tenth Ward was a wonderful melting pot, as my mother described it, with immigrants from other countries and migrants from the southern states. Russians, Jewish people, Germans, Czechoslovakians, Polish people, and African Americans lived there. Even then, I understood that there were artificial lines that black families could not cross to buy a home. And though we had an integrated neighborhood and integrated schools, our churches remained segregated.

Perhaps church segregation was more about culture and religious tradition than it was about race. The Russians worshiped in their Orthodox church, the Jews in their synagogue. Most Czechoslovakian and Polish neighbors were Catholic, the Germans were Lutheran, and the African Americans attended one of several black churches, including the Church of God, led by my grandfather, a lay pastor.

———————

Growing up, I learned that racism could come in subtle, surprising ways, even in my own church. As a young girl, I came to understand that I would never get to play the part of Mary in the Christmas pageant at my black church. A fair-skinned girl whose complexion looked like the familiar images of Jesus displayed in the church was always chosen to be Mary. The same light-skinned boy played Joseph each year too. The rest of us stood at the back or even offstage as darker-skinned members of the chorus. The funny thing is, I don't recall being resentful or angry. It was just one of those things I came to accept as part of life.

———————

One of my elementary school teachers asked our choral trio to sing at her Lutheran church in downtown Akron. On the morning we were to sing, we got off at the bus stop, walked up the church steps, and were greeted by a man with a quizzical look. He unsmilingly asked why we were there. When we told him that we had been invited to sing, he left for a moment then returned to say that no invitation had been extended. In the meantime, we had discovered that we were on the right street but at the wrong church. We had mistakenly gone to a different white Protestant congregation.

However, instead of sending us away, the man invited us to stay and sing.

It seemed a lovely gesture until the minister announced that "three colored girls" had come to share a song. I felt miffed that he had chosen to introduce us that way. Why didn't he just say that there were three young ladies who were going to sing? Our song was well received by the congregation, and my wounded feelings were soothed a bit when one of the church members invited us to stay after the service and share in their fellowship meal.

———•·•———

A year or two later when I was in high school, I auditioned for a citywide select choir. I prepared well and felt pleased with my audition performance. But when the names of the select choir were posted, I did not find my name on the list. Many of my fellow choir members were outwardly stunned, even angry that I had not been selected. I ran home, devastated by the news, and complained to my mother that I had not been selected because of my skin color. I had expected her to share my anger about the injustice of the situation. Instead, she said that perhaps I had sung too loudly or not on key. Or maybe I had not blended my voice with the others. I was terribly frustrated by my mother's unwillingness to acknowledge the racial bias. Later my heart was lifted when I discovered that I had been selected for the choir after all.

It appeared that the choir director had had a total change in attitude and bent over backward to include me.

Over a year passed before I discovered that my mother had gone to the high school principal to share her concern about the choir selection process. She didn't want me to know because she did not want to encourage me to use racism as an excuse for something that had gone wrong in my life. Instead of making a big scene, she quietly but effectively stood up to prejudice. It was a lesson I have tried to pass on to my children.

EXPERIENCING SEGREGATION IN THE MILITARY

On many occasions I felt the sting of rejection as a military wife. In 1949, Larry was stationed at Keesler Air Force Base. Since the military was segregated at the time, we were not allowed to live on base. We had rented a room with shared kitchen privileges in a black neighborhood in Biloxi, several miles from the base. At that point in history, a law stated that blacks and whites were not to cross a particular street separating the two racial groups. We were newlyweds, and we couldn't afford a car. The only way for Larry to get to the base was taking one of the segregated city buses, which were known as hotbeds of racial tension.

Two of Larry's white classmates at Keesler decided to defy the law. They took turns crossing the line, picking up Larry, and bringing him back home. Though I appreciated their kindness and courage, I couldn't help but worry. Each of them was taking a big risk, and I wondered what would have happened if they had been stopped.

On another occasion, we drove up to the gate at Perrin Air Force Base at Sherman, Texas, for a new assignment. It was late, we had traveled far, and we were tired. The soldier at the gate took a quick glance at Larry and announced that there was no base housing for us. He advised us to drive the sixty-five miles to Dallas. We scoured the streets of Big D looking for a motel that would accept us and finally landed in the only room we could find: a room in a bordello.

———•••———

During the time that Larry was stationed in Japan, I was the only black woman on base and often felt terribly lonely. When I was invited to participate in a bridge club with other military wives, I jumped at the opportunity, even though I was not an accomplished bridge player.

I had become a substitute teacher at the American Dependents School, and the school's principal was known as the best bridge player in the Officers' Wives Club. Over the course of a few weeks, I began to notice that when I was paired as the principal's partner or even playing at the same table, her game somehow seemed off-kilter. It became obvious that she was distracted, and I was pretty sure it was because of me.

Over time, the principal and I each transitioned from the school to the base's education office where we continued to develop a friendship. One day while having coffee together, she opened up about what she had been feeling during our first encounters playing bridge.

"When I was growing up, there were always colored people in my home, but I never had to socialize with them," she said.

She went on to explain that she had been raised in Georgia during the days of racial segregation. Her family had employed a number of black household workers. She was accustomed to having African Americans on the backstage of her life but not as her equals. Then she said something that gave me pause. She confessed that she'd had an aunt who often said that if she got to heaven and there were colored people there, she'd rather go to hell.

I actually felt encouraged by this woman's honesty. I tried to imagine what it would have been like to have been in her shoes, raised in an environment where hatred and skewed perceptions were deeply ingrained in her life from a young age. I was also grateful that my mother had helped me understand that if you focus on building relationships, the walls of prejudice eventually will come tumblin' down.

We were living at a base in Arizona a few years after that. I was admitted to the base hospital earlier than expected to give birth to our second child, Sally-Ann. I remember being wheeled to the end of an open ward, far away from the nearest white patient. The nurse quickly drew the curtain, not as if she wanted to protect my privacy but as if she were somehow protecting the white patients from me.

As we passed the white patients, I couldn't help but hear them talk. They unashamedly questioned how my African-American husband could be a pilot. One person even critiqued my clothing. I stewed silently. Apparently I was not only invisible—I was deaf too.

———•———

Contrary to what many believe, racial prejudice did not happen just in the South. When we were stationed in Sioux City, Iowa, our family went into a local restaurant and sat down. We soon noticed that others who had come in after we did had already been served their food. Still no one came to our table to offer a menu or a glass of water. Finally we realized that the management had no intention of serving us. So with all eyes on our family, we quietly slipped out of our seats and left the cafe.

Not long after the experience in the cafe, another military wife encouraged me to enroll Sally-Ann in the preschool program in Sioux City. June, a white woman from Texas, the wife of another pilot, had become my friend, and I was excited about the possibility of our children going to preschool together. My excitement, however, was short-lived. When June inquired about enrolling Sally-Ann, the director curtly told her that African-American children were not accepted into the program.

Thankfully, at her young age, Sally-Ann was not aware of the preschool rejection, but it wasn't long before she felt the pang of racism firsthand. The family who lived behind us on the base had a birthday party for their daughter in the backyard area we neighbors all shared. Every child on base was invited, every child except Sally-Ann. It was a heartbreaking scene, watching her disappointment as she looked out the window to see other children gathering without her.

While the party was in progress, a white Norwegian woman was helping me clean the windows of our home. A few days later, the neighbor who'd hosted the party noticed my sparkling windows. When she saw the woman working outside my home, the neighbor came over to ask if she had a day that she could clean the windows of her home.

The Norwegian woman frowned, put her hands on her hips, and spoke to my neighbor with a thick accent and serious tone, "If I had any days, I wouldn't give them to you! Not after what you did to my little one." I have a feeling my neighbor was shocked to hear the woman refer to Sally-Ann as her little one. Even so, the reprimand must have pricked my neighbor's conscience. She eventually apologized for her thoughtlessness. Though I was grateful for her apology, my daughter's heart had already been broken.

We left Sioux City for an assignment back in Tuskegee, Alabama; and on our way, we made a stop in Nashville,

Tennessee. We went into a hotel restaurant near Fisk University, a black university in that city. Larry and I were stunned when Sally-Ann stepped into the restaurant and happily announced, "Everybody in here is my color!" It was a moment of innocent amazement. Knowing that she had been the only black child among her playmates in Iowa, we couldn't help but wonder if she had always felt different because of her color.

Sometimes people want to know of all the places we lived during Larry's military service, which one was my favorite. I can honestly say that each assignment held enjoyable experiences, but I always had a preference for Tuskegee, Alabama. As I think back on it, Tuskegee is an unlikely choice considering that it was so highly segregated when we were there in the late 1950s and early 1960s.

Actually, Larry was not keen on leaving his position as a jet pilot policing the Canadian-U.S. corridor during the Cold War to move to the South and become an ROTC instructor at the Tuskegee Institute, a historically black school first led by Booker T. Washington. But when you are in the military, you follow orders. So we piled into our Rambler station wagon, with the luggage tied on top and covered with a tarpaulin, and drove from Iowa to Alabama.

After a short stay in a cramped two-bedroom apartment, our family of five settled into a house on Roberts Circle, an amusing coincidence of names, we thought. It seemed that for the first time in their young lives, our older children had the opportunity to interact with other children of their color. My heart overflowed to see them flourish in their new environment. Butch performed in his first operetta and was a member of safety patrol. Sally-Ann was elected Miss Valentine, and I devoted a lot of time to the Parent Teachers Association. Our family became active in Greenwood Missionary Baptist Church, where I sang in the choir and served on the flower committee, considered quite an honor. Larry took advantage of being on campus to begin work on his master's degree. Every member of the family, including little Dorothy, our youngest at the time, seemed happy living in this black community, in spite of the racial injustice that hemmed us in.

One highlight of our time at Tuskegee came late one summer day when Martin Luther King Jr. came to the Institute to speak about nonviolent protests in the face of local racial injustices. Larry insisted that we get to the gymnasium early because he knew there would be a massive crowd. He took the two older children and sat in the bleachers while I sat on the floor in a beat-up green lawn chair we'd brought from home. I positioned the chair at the back of the room so that I could corral Dorothy, an active toddler. Although I couldn't hear everything Dr. King said, I heard him at the moment when he began to sing an old spiritual, "In Bright Mansions." It was the first time I had ever heard that song.

The crowd immediately joined in, and their words wafted through the stifling air of summer:

In Bright Mansions

In bright mansions above
Lord, I wan' t' live up yonder
In bright mansions above

I sat in awe while everyone filed out of the room in thoughtful silence.

Because of the presence of Tuskegee Institute, blacks made up the majority of Tuskegee's population. However, almost all of the businesses were owned by whites, many of whom considered blacks to be second-class citizens. City leaders feared the increasing number of black voter registrants and sought to redraw city boundaries as a way of keeping blacks from participating in leadership positions.

Not long after Dr. King's appearance on campus, the only black-owned grocery store in Tuskegee mysteriously burned to the ground, making a tense atmosphere even more unsettling. Campus administrators kept a concerned eye on the students, fearing that their passion might spill over into aggression. Instead, students organized and led a peaceful, silent march into downtown Tuskegee.

After the march, we were told to expect retaliation from the Ku Klux Klan. As a security precaution, all of the lights on campus were turned off, creating an eerie darkness that enveloped us. We complied with instructions to move into the interior of the house, away from windows, where we huddled together as a family. It was a frightening time, particularly for a mother of young children. Thankfully, nothing happened to us or to our home that night, but the apprehension most certainly did not vanish at daybreak.

In another protest, the black community began a boycott of white-owned businesses that were not friendly to blacks. It lasted four years and caused economic difficulty for the local businesses. Though it was inconvenient to travel the forty miles to Montgomery to buy food and clothing, there was solidarity among all of us in the Tuskegee Institute community. We understood that the boycott fulfilled Dr. King's idea of a nonviolent but effective way to stand up to injustice.

Before one particular trip to Montgomery, Larry and I discussed whether we should try to explain to Butch about segregated water fountains. We finally decided against any explanation, thinking that he would not likely ask for a drink of water. However, once we were in the store, Butch immediately ran to a water fountain and read the sign designating it a colored water fountain. To our amazement, he looked at us and abruptly announced, "This water's not colored!"

It is fair to say that our time in Tuskegee was both the best and worst of times. We felt at home. We savored family time on the screened-in porch where Campus, the affectionate stray dog we adopted, liked to nap. With Robin's birth in November of 1960, our family was complete. Tuskegee was a place of warm, wonderful memories, yet the volatile nature of prejudice was never far from our minds. In fact, it was only steps away from campus.

———•◦•———

During the early years of integrating the military, I sometimes was the only officer's wife not invited to an event. Being the only black woman in the organization, it was easy to feel alone, excluded, and marginalized. I learned to orchestrate the situation by quietly asserting myself in the proper role of an officer's wife. I had practically memorized a book of protocol for officers' wives. I would show up wearing my hat, white gloves, and a gracious smile. I even kept an extra pair of white gloves in my purse in case the first pair got soiled.

I admit it was difficult to thrust myself into situations where some people did not want me. Often conversations would cease when I walked into the room. I kept reminding myself that Larry had earned every promotion he received, and I had my dignity and self-respect to uphold too. Or maybe I had just found my voice by refusing to be defined by another's warped attitude.

When Larry was assigned to an Air Force base in Arizona, we found at least six other black officers there. I had not realized how much I had missed the company of other women of color until then. One of the wives was a former Howard University classmate, so we had much in common. It was refreshing to be part of a sisterhood. We shopped together at Goldwater's and laughed over coffee. I found comfort in being with women who shared similar life experiences.

———•◦•———

In the 1970s, Larry was serving in Vietnam while the rest of our family remained behind in Biloxi. I was invited to attend a women's prayer group. I remember feeling my blackness acutely among these white women. One woman in particular kept staring at me. I could sense that the other women noticed too and felt uncomfortable with her obsession over me. As the only black woman in the group, I tried not to let it bother me, but it was a challenge to concentrate on prayer with this woman's eyes constantly fixed on me.

Several weeks later, I answered my front door and discovered the woman who had been staring at me. She was holding a poinsettia and extended it toward me. I invited her inside, and though she seemed a little uncertain, she stepped into my home. After a brief moment, she made a confession.

"I feel right with God except for this one thing," she said, referring to her racial bias. "I want you to know something. I have come to love you."

It seems that during our prayer time together, she had been confronted by her own racist attitude. Gratefully, she had come to more fully understand that we are called to love one another in Christ. It was a humbling experience, both for her and for me.

————•◦•————

Jesus Loves the Little Children

Jesus loves the little children,
All the children of the world.
Red and yellow, black and white,
All are precious in his sight,
Jesus loves the little children of the world.

EPHESIANS 2:10
We are God's handiwork,
created in Christ Jesus to do good works,
which God prepared in advance for us to do.

Robin's *Reflection*

My mom and I haven't always seen eye to eye when it comes to race. In fact, when I was much younger, I often rolled my eyes when the subject came up with her. But as I matured I realized that Mom grew up in a different time and faced discrimination I could only imagine. Yet she always looks for the good in people . . . and has always been one to teach that life is not all black and white.

A memory I cherish is watching Mom at President Barack Obama's inauguration. It was below freezing that day, but Mom was there in her mink coat that she bought at a rummage sale for $25 in 1967. I saw tears glistening in her beautiful brown eyes—transfixed—as she witnessed the first African-American commander in chief take the oath of office. She thought she'd never see that in her lifetime. We all wished Dad had lived to see this day too.

Chapter 4

"ANGELS" WATCHING OVER ME

I have often wondered what direction my life might have taken without the influence of certain individuals, especially Wilma Schnegg. Miss Schnegg was a woman of German heritage who taught at Robinson Elementary School in Akron. When I was in the second grade, Miss Schnegg would stand at the classroom door and smile at each child who entered. I always looked forward to the way she would flash her lovely smile then gently pat the top of my head. Actually, she repeated the scene for every child who came into her room, but I remember how extraordinary it made me feel.

Miss Schnegg, a gifted educator, made storybook characters come alive for me. At the same time, her calm demeanor could quiet a group of rowdy children with just a raised eyebrow. But the thing I remember most fondly about Miss

Schnegg was her nonjudgmental attitude. Every day she just exuded warmth and acceptance.

Long after I had moved from second grade to the upper grade levels, I realized that Miss Schnegg was still taking a special interest in me. When I would perform in a pageant or concert at school, I would look up from the stage to see Miss Schnegg standing in the back of the auditorium with an affirming grin on her face. If I passed her in the hall at school, she would call me by name and ask me about my classes. It seemed that no matter where I went, Miss Schnegg turned up somewhere close by, always with a genuine interest and an encouraging word.

In the spring of my eighth-grade year, the time came to register for the classes that I would take as a freshman in high school. Most of my friends signed up for the least-rigorous classes because that was all that was expected. I was about to follow suit when Miss Schnegg sought me out to review my class selections. In her quiet but firm way, Miss Schnegg directed me to the more challenging college-preparatory classes, including Latin and algebra, speech and chemistry. Though I could barely believe her words, she kept insisting that I was going to college. It was the first time anyone had dared to mention college as a possibility for my life.

Even after I had left elementary school and was a student at Akron's East High School, Miss Schnegg seemed to appear at just the right time to help me select classes for the following year. At times I wondered whether Miss Schnegg was teaming up with my principal, Mr. A. J. Dillehay, to keep a watchful eye over me. Miss Schnegg talked confidently about financial scholarships and the importance of maintaining good grades. I was keenly aware that my family could not afford to send me to college, but Miss Schnegg had planted the seed of possibility in my mind and helped me to envision a future much bigger than I had ever imagined.

Then during my junior year of high school, Mr. Dillehay introduced me to a recruiter for Howard University who was touring our campus. At the time, I didn't know much about Howard except that it was a well-respected, historically black university in Washington, DC. I was elated when Mr. Dillehay told the recruiter that Howard University should be interested in recruiting me. Just hearing those words gave me a huge boost of confidence. For months afterward, I kept replaying the exchange in my mind, hearing that Lucimarian Tolliver was someone Howard University should be interested in!

About the same time, Miss Schnegg made me aware of the John S. Knight scholarships given by the founders of the *Akron Beacon Journal* newspaper to students who had proved themselves academically, showed leadership qualities, and passed the college entrance exam. The application process required writing an essay about what university I wanted to attend and why I wanted to go there. My mind immediately raced back to the comment that Mr. Dillehay had made to the recruiter almost a year earlier. So I wrote about Howard

University and my desire to study social work there. I also knew that if I attended Howard, it would be the first time in my school career that I would be taught by black teachers. I had to admit, I found the idea intriguing.

I was invited to sing "God Bless America" at my high school graduation. Preparing to sing, I looked out across the sea of faces and saw Miss Schnegg standing at the back of the auditorium as she had done so many other times. I've often wondered what she had seen in young Lucimarian Tolliver that prompted her to invest so much of herself in my future.

FOLLOWING GOOD ROLE MODELS

Along life's journey, there have been other people who took me under their wing and selflessly gave their time and talents to mentor me. Several were the wives of black professionals from the Akron area. One woman was the wife of the first black postal carrier in our area. At the time, the local Young Women's Christian Association did not allow young black girls to participate in its programs. It seemed so contradictory for a Christian organization not to allow Christian girls of color into its membership. This woman quietly took action and prevailed upon the YWCA to offer a room where black girls from high schools across Akron could participate in our own leadership program.

In her efforts to convince the administrators, the woman specifically pointed to the honors many of us had achieved in our own high schools. I was pleased that she noted my leadership on East High's student council and in the National Honor Society. She persisted until finally the YWCA agreed to her request, allowing us to use a room in the YWCA for a leadership program. It may have been a minor victory, but that victory opened the door enough to eventually integrate the YWCA in our area.

The wife of a local attorney also took a special interest in me and other young black women. She was a wonderful mother to three sons, but she had a strong desire to nurture black teenage girls. She would load up a group of us girls and drive us to Wilberforce University, a black university in Ohio. On campus, we would interact with the black students, watch their tennis matches, and attend an occasional garden show sponsored by the university. As Miss Schnegg had done by planting the idea of college in my mind, this mentor opened our eyes to new possibilities too.

Another event involving this woman sticks in my mind. One day she stopped at the counter in Woolworth's to have lunch but was told that it was against the law for her to eat there. She knew the law and calmly reminded the management that they could not refuse her service because of her color. The employees became so angry that they started breaking the china plates. She said she couldn't help but giggle at their ridiculous response, so she encouraged other black shoppers to go inside and order lunch too, even offering to pay for it herself. "They are breaking plates in Woolworth's!"

she announced, adding that it wouldn't be long until Woolworth's was out of plates! This woman was a mentor who impressed upon me the value of humor and courage in the face of prejudice.

Yet another woman who unselfishly gave her time and talent to me was the wife of a local dentist. She shared my love of music and often made recommendations for spirituals or hymns she thought I would enjoy. Many times when I sang for services or events around town, this woman graciously volunteered to play the accompaniment for me.

From the parents of my childhood friend Wanda Jones I learned important lessons about radical hospitality. In many ways, Wanda was like an older sister to me. On most mornings, I would walk to Wanda's house, then we would go to school together.

I will never forget the aroma of hot biscuits and sausage prepared for us by Wanda's mother. Thinking back, I realize I must have been another mouth to feed during bad economic times. Gratefully, Wanda's father was able to maintain a good job, which made their lives a little easier. But always, Wanda's family made me feel welcome in their home.

Later Mrs. Jones told the story that whenever she would ask if I wanted to stay for a meal, I would respond demurely, "Well, I don't care." I suppose it was my attempt to be polite. In reality, I'm certain that Mrs. Jones knew I was anxious to share their family meal. To this day I can still taste Mrs. Jones's heavenly butterscotch pie, a favorite Sunday dessert.

Finding Friends in Time of Need

Throughout Larry's military service, it always seemed that there were neighbors and friends who looked after us. No matter where we lived, we encountered people who modeled lives of compassion and community. What impressed me most was that people who barely knew us often carried out these acts of kindness.

After we were turned away from base housing in Sherman, Texas, a black office worker happened to overhear a conversation Larry had with the administrators. As Larry was leaving, she followed him down the hall and quietly pulled him aside. She invited our family to temporarily share her family's home in a black community in a sister city, Denison, Texas. Her husband was being transferred in three weeks. After that, she said we could rent the house for our family.

Oh, how that community embraced us even though we lived there less than six months! My neighbor's kitchen window faced mine, and sometimes I would hear a tap on her glass—her signal that she had baked something to share with our family. I also remember one hot summer day when I was five-months pregnant. I had gone outside with a laundry cart filled with clothes, but soon the scorching heat overwhelmed me. I left the cart and went back inside to rest. It wasn't long before I started receiving phone calls from every neighbor within sight of my cart, each checking to see if I was all right.

Shortly after we arrived in Denison, Larry and I made friends with a school principal and his wife. I will never forget their kindness when Larry received a new assignment, and I had to stay behind with Butch to pack up the house and prepare to move again. The principal and his wife invited us to stay at their home after the movers had taken our belongings. They even got up in the middle of the night to take us to the station where we caught our train to Arizona.

While stationed in Sioux City, Iowa, I experienced the same sense of community among families we had only recently met. On one particular Saturday morning, Larry and a fellow pilot, one of our neighbors, had a flight assignment. Sally-Ann and Butch were playing in the yard with a group of kids when I looked out the kitchen window and saw a huge plume of black smoke. My heart dropped, knowing there had been a crash and fearing the worst.

On such occasions, Larry had always called to let me know that he was okay. This time the phone did not ring. I tried to remain calm, especially since I was pregnant with our third child. Still the phone did not ring.

Soon my neighbor June came over to tell me that she had spoken with her husband, Bob, a pilot working on the base line that morning. He had asked her to stay with me because the officials weren't sure if the crashed plane had been piloted by Larry or by our neighbor, Dick.

June remained by my side throughout the ordeal, keeping an eye on the children and trying to distract my thoughts from time to time. It wasn't long before we saw the chaplain's blue car edging toward us. June and I looked at each other and took in a deep breath. It was a bittersweet moment when we watched the chaplain's car pull into Dick's driveway, not ours.

I prayed for Dick's family, including his children who had been playing outside with mine. At the same time, I was relieved it had not been Larry. Perhaps not surprisingly, I went into labor that night. Our car was low on gas since we did not expect the baby to arrive early. Bob and June were going to watch our older children and offered us their car. But when we got in, it wouldn't start. So we returned to our car and said a prayer that we would have enough gas to get to the hospital. Thankfully we did, and our daughter Dorothy arrived two weeks early.

There was another time in Sioux City when Larry was away on an assignment for several days. I came down with a terrible case of the flu that caused me to shiver uncontrollably. Sally-Ann, just a preschooler, went next door to June's house and announced that her mommy was sick. Within a few hours, June had organized the neighbors to help care for the children and to provide a full meal for each night until I was well. As miserable as I felt at the time, I basked in the good feelings of a community caring for one another.

The Cold War escalated during the years we spent at Sioux City. Military families were subjected to increasing fear and stress. As always, I turned to my faith for comfort and encouragement.

Though I had known chaplains from the various bases where Larry had served, the chaplain at Sioux City, Chaplain Deutschlander, acted as a distinctly calming and reassuring presence during this challenging season of life. He would slip into a back row seat and listen to our choir rehearsal. Afterward, he would offer a soothing word to diffuse the tension we were all feeling.

Chaplain Deutschlander was an ordained Lutheran minister. One day he suggested that it was time for a service of blessing for our third child, Dorothy, who had been born just a few weeks before. Following the service, Rev. Deutschlander and his wife, Helmie, invited us to their home in the countryside. As was their custom, they met us at the door with a tray of filled wine glasses. As soon as eight-year-old Butch saw the wine glasses, he backed away and threw his hands in the air, boldly telling the chaplain, "I don't drink." We were both proud and tickled by Butch's rebuff.

RECEIVING WISDOM AND CARE
FROM FRIENDS

I have to confess that over the thirty-two-year span of Larry's Air Force career, there were moments when the burden of making another move seemed more than I could bear. One time I just wanted to call it quits. Thankfully a former Howard University classmate stepped into my life at just the right moment.

Larry and I had decided to build a home in a new Tuskegee subdivision. Larry was nearing the twenty-year mark in his career, and I thought he was going to retire and take a job that would allow us to stay in one location. We signed a contract and put down a deposit for a new house. Then one day, on the spur of the moment, I decided to drop by and talk with the developer about a few questions. I was shocked to discover that Larry had cancelled the contract and reclaimed our deposit!

I could feel my anger about to erupt like molten lava. How dare he make that decision without me! Shortly after I had met the contractor, my Howard classmate and sorority sister Cannie came to my home for coffee. Her husband also had been assigned to Tuskegee. I found myself ranting and raving about Larry, something I usually did not do. I told her I was not going to put up with his behavior and that I was going to leave Larry.

Calm and rational, Cannie listened patiently without judging or encouraging me. Then she quietly asked a series of questions that caused me to stop and think. Where would I go? What about the children? How would we live?

In a matter of minutes, the lava quit spewing. As angry as I had been, I admitted that I had married Larry because I loved him, and I loved him still. Larry later gave me a litany of logical reasons for cancelling the contract, none of which really satisfied me; but I chose to take a step on the path to forgiveness.

Reflecting on that story now, I feel slightly amused. Many years later, I did almost the same thing that Larry had done to me. By then he had retired from the Air Force after more than thirty years, and we had decided that in addition to our home in Pass Christian, it would be helpful to rent an apartment near the medical facilities at Keesler Air Force Base in Biloxi. As we were aging, we were making many more trips to the doctor. Also we were traveling for various church and board meetings, so a small apartment close to the airport and to Keesler's medical facilities made perfect sense. It would be a place to stay when we needed to be close by for medical and travel purposes.

One Sunday afternoon I left Larry watching football on TV while I went to Biloxi to tour an apartment we had seen advertised. From the photographs, it appeared lovely, just the right size and price that would work well for us as a second home. On my way to see the apartment, my eyes were drawn to a beautiful entrance into an intimate neighborhood of gracious homes set on wooded lots in Biloxi. I spied one with a For Sale sign. The house featured French doors and a wide front porch that reminded me of my childhood home. Then and there I think I dismissed the apartment idea. In fact, I never even drove by the apartment.

I drove straight home and told Larry about the house for sale. He looked at me as if I had lost my mind. Begrudgingly, he went with me to see the house the next day, grumbling about why in the world we were looking at a house instead of an apartment. After touring the home, he was shocked when I boldly announced to the realtor that we wanted to make an offer. Larry and I hadn't discussed it, and I didn't even know the asking price!

After a few days, we negotiated a deal on the house. Larry even grew to enjoy it as our second home. I once told him that I thought God had directed me to that house. He immediately responded that he didn't think God had intended for us to have two mortgages! Even as we laughed about it later, I haven't forgotten the way that Cannie made me stop and think that day in Tuskegee.

Larry and I were not exempt from stubborn wills that sometimes collided. All of us are flawed people. All of us make mistakes. Thankfully, though, we both knew that in a great marriage two flawed people are brought back into unity through the grace of God.

"For I was hungry and you gave me something to eat, I was thirsty and you gave me something to drink, I was a stranger and you invited me in." These words from the Gospel of Matthew rang true for me during the trying time after Larry died. Because of health issues, I lived temporarily in an assisted living center near Robin's home in Connecticut. I found being away from all that was familiar in Mississippi disconcerting. On weekends when Robin was away on an assignment, one of her friends, Gretchen Fuchs, would take me to church and out for brunch.

Another of Robin's friends, Ellen Walsh, visited me each week in the assisted living center and took me out to lunch. She often brought me books to read and would ask thoughtful questions about my life. After one of our conversations, Ellen returned the following week with a census document about my great-grandfather, Matthew Tolliver, who had been a slave in Shepherdstown, West Virginia. She even found a postcard of the children's home where I worked when I first graduated from Howard. In a hard season of life, I was the stranger. Gretchen and Ellen invited me into their lives, and I am grateful.

———•◦•———

Over the span of my years, people of all different ages and races have encouraged and mentored me along the way. Their lives have intersected with mine at the precise moment I needed them most. Each one, in ways big and small, altered the trajectory of my life. The only way I know to repay them is to pass it on.

Blessed Assurance

Blessed assurance, Jesus is mine!
O what a foretaste of glory divine!
Heir of salvation, purchase of God,
born of his Spirit, washed in his blood.

This is my story, this is my song,
praising my Savior all the day long;
this is my story, this is my song,
praising my Savior all the day long.

---

1 PETER 5:2-3

Be shepherds of God's flock that is under your care,
watching over them—not because you must,
but because you are willing, as God wants you to be;
not pursuing dishonest gain, but eager to serve;
not lording it over those entrusted to you,
but being examples to the flock.

Robin's *Reflection*

Mom appreciates the awards she has received for her good works but always insists the recognition should go to someone else. She frequently points out the many people God has put in her path to guide her. I have often heard the stories of these angels. Little did they know that they would change not only Mom's life but also the lives of her children.

None of us gets where we are on our own. I'll never forget the time I lost sight of that for a moment. Thankfully, my mother was there to remind me. In the early 1990s, I gave a commencement speech at the University of Southern Mississippi. My mother was in the audience. In my speech I talked about the things I had done, what I had learned, how I'd coped with adversity, and the importance of following your passion.

After the speech, I noticed that my mother was completely quiet. I finally said, "What's the problem?"

She just looked at me, then she said, "Do you know how many people have helped you? When you were standing up there, it wasn't just you. It was your teachers, your coaches, your mentors. . . ."

I listened to her words and I felt ashamed. . . . It was one of the few times my mother had ever expressed disappointment in me. Her words stung, but they were true. Thankfully it's a mistake I have never made again.

Left:
Elizabeth and George
Suddeth, Lucimarian's
maternal grandparents,
circa 1929

Right:
Lucimarian with son,
Butch, and a friend in
Japan, circa 1952

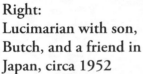

Left:
Robin and Lucimarian
at the recording studio
where Lucimarian taped
a CD of her favorite
hymns and spirituals
as a gift to her family in
2011

Left:
Lucimarian's mother, Sally, standing, in white dress, with siblings circa 1946 in Akron, Ohio. Sally's mother is seated. The Tolliver siblings left to right: George, Lucille, Bill, Mary, Sally, Henry, Jim, Tom

Right:
Sally Suddeth Tolliver, Lucimarian's mother

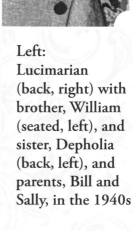

Left:
Lucimarian (back, right) with brother, William (seated, left), and sister, Depholia (back, left), and parents, Bill and Sally, in the 1940s

Above: Lucimarian and Butch
in Japan, 1950s

Below: Lucimarian in Japan
during cherry blossom time
in 1951

Above: Lucimarian with her mother
and son, Butch, in Akron, Ohio

Below: Lucimarian's husband,
Larry, a flight instructor at Tuskegee
Institute in the 1960s

Right:
Lucimarian and
daughter Dorothy
at the inauguration
of the first
African-American
President of the
United States,
Barack Obama,
January 20, 2009

Above:
Lucimarian's mentor, Miss
Wilma Schnegg, left, with
family members, 1953

Right:
Lucimarian sent this photo to
Larry Roberts who was serving
in the military circa 1943

Above: Larry and Lucimarian Roberts at a military event

Below: Graduation from Howard University, 1946

Above: Singing at Howard prepared Lucimarian for later performances. She sang "I Could Have Danced All Night" at a 1958 PTA fundraiser in Tuskegee.

Right:
Robin receives honorary doctorate from Howard University, May 2010. Accompanied by Dorothy, Sally-Ann, and Lucimarian.

Left:
In 1997 Larry, Lucimarian, Sally-Ann, Dorothy, and Robin visited the church they had attended when stationed in Izmir, Turkey many years before.

Left:
Larry Roberts in dress uniform, 1970s

Right:
Larry Roberts as a member of the Army Air Corps circa 1945

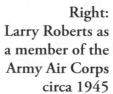

Left:
Lucimarian looking to the future before the move to Japan, circa 1951

Below:
Larry and Lucimarian board the ferry to Robben Island to tour Mandela's prison, 2004

Below:
1997 trip to Turkey and Greece: Robin, Lucimarian, Larry, Dorothy, and Sally-Ann

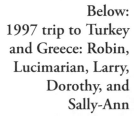

Right:
Lucimarian at the Cape of Good Hope while on family trip to South Africa, 2004

Above/Left: Larry was one of the original Tuskegee Airmen. He was awarded the Congressional Medal of Honor posthumously by President George W. Bush.

Right:
Three generations of Roberts men: Lawrence II (Butch) and son, Lawrence III, flank Lawrence I (Larry) Roberts, in 2001

Left: Lucimarian's 85th birthday celebration. Lucimarian surrounded by son, Butch, and daughters, Sally-Ann, Dorothy, and Robin.

Chapter 5

STEPPING OUT
OF THE BUBBLE

There was a strict Sunday morning rule in my childhood home: no one was to open the newspaper until we had returned from church. So when I arrived at Sunday school as a high school senior one morning in 1942, I was unprepared for the congratulatory cheers coming from church members. They had already seen my name and photograph in the *Akron Beacon Journal* newspaper, announcing me as the winner of a John S. Knight scholarship. All I could think was that Miss Schnegg's advice and encouragement had paid off!

For the next few hours I quivered with impatience before finally racing home after the last amen. I was anxious to see the announcement in my own copy of the newspaper. For some reason it seemed as though it might not be true until I saw it with my own eyes.

I quickly scanned through the pages until I found it. There it was: my photo with the announcement. Lucimarian Tolliver, graduating senior at East High School in Akron. Scholarship winner. It seemed a dream, at once lovely and nebulous. Who in their wildest imagination would have thought that I would be going to college?

The summer months slipped by quickly. I was employed as a domestic worker for a family who owned a jewelry store, then as a check clerk at a five-and-dime store, trying to save as much money as I could for college. Just a few days before I was to board the train to go from Akron to Washington, DC, my family hosted a send-off party for me. Family members filled my parents' home with their soaring spirits and high expectations. Being the first person in my family to go to college, I felt tremendous pride. But the gratification mingled with a heavy sense of responsibility. I did not want to disappoint those who were placing their hopes and dreams in me. All during the afternoon's festivities, family members slipped me envelopes with notes of good wishes along with some of their hard-earned cash.

As the party ended, everyone formed a circle around me and held hands. We stood silent for a moment. Then one by one, family members began to pray for me, starting with my grandmother. My heart was tendered.

The morning after the party, my festive mood was momentarily disrupted when my mother reminded me that before I left for Howard, I should visit my grandfather who had been unable to attend the party because of his deteriorating health. I loved my grandfather dearly, but he could be quite intimidating. He was a tall man, an imposing figure in spite of involuntary tremors caused by Parkinson's disease. On this day, his facial expression was serious, as usual.

I recall that his mouth tightened with passion as he said, "Be very careful of the friends you select at college. You have been raised with Christian standards. Look for friends who will live up to those standards, and steer clear of those who won't. And never lower your standards."

My grandfather's eyes remained fixed on mine for what seemed an eternity. He must have been thinking about how sheltered I had been, growing up in this melting-pot neighborhood. He probably wondered if I was really prepared for the world outside Akron because he understood all too well the temptations and challenges that awaited me.

LEAVING THE NEST

Packing for the unknown experience of college turned into a family affair. Earlier in the summer, my mother had received a list of items I would need for my dorm room, including a blanket, towels, pillow, and bed linens. My father found an old trunk, which I filled with my clothes. Before my mother was able to pack the bed linens in the trunk, my father called the railway express and had the trunk picked up. When my mother questioned his actions, he said I could just wrap the bed linens in brown paper, tie them with twine, and check them on the train as luggage. He was wrong.

When I arrived at the train station, I was filled with excitement laced with a certain amount of fear. I was also toting a bulky stack of brown paper packages that did not qualify as luggage. I had to find space to squeeze them in the overhead bins.

It didn't take long before I discovered that I was supposed to have made a reservation for a seat in the coach section of the train. I had expected to pay for a ticket once on board, but when the porter came by to collect tickets, he explained that I would have to move to the smoker car.

Perhaps it was a God-incidence that I had taken a seat next to Mamie Hansberry, another incoming Howard University student, whose father was accompanying her to Washington. As soon as Mr. Hansberry understood my situation, he graciously surrendered his seat and went to the smoker car, allowing me to sit with Mamie for the duration of the train ride to Washington. I have often wondered if divine intervention was again at play when Mamie turned out to be my freshman roommate at Howard.

Except for Mamie and her father, I arrived at Howard University alone and naïve. I soon learned that many of the students were from wealthy homes in the south or from metropolitan areas like Chicago and New York. Their parents, typically professionals such as doctors, attorneys, and business owners, hovered around the students as they unloaded trunks filled with belongings. Though we were all young black students, I already felt different.

How I wished that my mother could have been there to help me get settled in, but the cost of an additional train ticket was too much. Even with my scholarship, money was tight. Later, when classmates asked what my father did for a living, I simply smiled and repeated what my longtime friend Wanda had taught me to say: he was a commissioner. According to Wanda, there were many different kinds of commissioners, and the students at Howard didn't need to know what kind of commissioner my father was.

During the following months, I learned that college differed quite a bit from my life in Akron's Tenth Ward. For the first time I was surrounded by classmates who smoked and drank. Most of them showed little interest in church, which made the words of my grandfather percolate through my mind.

On some days I felt quite inferior to my more worldly classmates. I remember being so proud of the new plaid skirt and solid-colored jacket, white socks, and penny loafers I had bought with my hard-earned money. During the summer, while perusing the pages of *Mademoiselle* magazine I had seen a model wearing similar clothes. I purchased an outfit, thinking I would surely fit in with the latest fashion trends on campus. I curled my hair into a pageboy and secured it with a barrette. To my surprise, it seemed I was the only young woman in penny loafers and socks. Most of the others wore dress shoes and hose. And when weather turned cold, other young women suddenly appeared in luxurious fur coats, while I wrapped myself in a brown teddy bear coat trimmed in green with a matching kelly green cloche.

LIFE-SHAPING INFLUENCES

Everywhere I looked, the Howard University campus seemed to overflow with extremely attractive young black women. I was beginning to feel quite insecure when something happened that brought me back to my senses. My psychology class was visiting an area psychiatric hospital. One of the patients looked at the group of beautiful women, then boldly asked, "Is there a Mary McLeod Bethune among you?"

My classmates looked around, bewildered, but I immediately understood what the patient meant. He was referring to Dr. Bethune, the well-respected educator and highest ranking black person in President Franklin Roosevelt's administration. She also served as the director of the Division of Negro Affairs of the National Youth Administration.

The patient's question jolted me and also intrigued me. He really wanted to know whether there was a woman of substance and integrity among the beautiful women in the room. Was there someone not so consumed with her appearance that she would invest her life in the lives of others? A Mary McLeod Bethune. I never lost sight of that patient's wisdom. In fact, today I belong to an organization of black women who recite a passage from Mary McLeod Bethune's "My Last Will and Testament" at each meeting. That essay lifts up the values of love, hope, education, dignity, and responsibility to young people, among several others.

On another occasion at Howard, I made an offhand comment to a friend about the number of stunning women on the university campus. Dean Warner Lawson overheard my remark, turned, and gave me a weighty stare before quietly saying, "But Lucimarian, they don't have your character." Even after all these years, I am reminded of Dean Warner's words whenever I find myself putting too much emphasis on physical beauty.

Not long after I had arrived on campus my freshman year, the resident director summoned us girls in the very early morning when it was still dark outside. Having been aroused from a deep sleep, we were groggy, confused, and chatty. I remember the dorm mentors standing at the end of each hall, shushing us as we made our way downstairs.

When we arrived in the gathering area, we were instructed to sit on the floor. The dean of Rankin Chapel, Dr. Howard Thurman, arrived and began to speak. I don't think I had ever heard such a magnificent speaking voice. He recited these lines from "Still, Still with Thee," written by Harriet Beecher Stowe:

Still, Still with Thee

Still, still with Thee, when purple morning breaketh,
When the bird waketh, and the shadows flee;
Fairer than morning, lovelier than daylight,
Dawns the sweet consciousness, I am with Thee.

Dr. Thurman gave a wonderful message about being still and listening to the voice of God, commanding a sense of reverence and awe. He concluded just as the sun began inching its way into the sky, splashing a soft golden light across the room. My heart was moved as we left in silence.

———•-•-•———

Though many of my peers shied away from participating in Dr. Thurman's chapel services, I was drawn to the comfort and renewal I found there. Wednesday night chapel helped center me for another week. There was a hymn singing followed by warm, buttery popcorn and hot cider in the basement. I loved singing with the chapel choir and was touched when Dr. Thurman attended a rehearsal and heard me sing a solo in "Rockin' Jerusalem." To my delight, Dr. Thurman later commented how much he liked my solo. His words sounded like music to my eager, freshman ears.

Rockin' Jerusalem

O Mary, O Martha,
O Mary, ring dem bells.

O Mary, O Martha,
O Mary, ring dem bells.

I hear archangels a-rockin' Jerusalem,
I hear archangels a-ringin' dem bells.

Church gettin' higher! Rockin' Jerusalem!
Church gettin' higher! Ringin' dem bells.
New Jerusalem! Rockin' Jerusalem!
New Jerusalem! Ringin' dem bells.

———•—•———

Dr. Warner Lawson, dean of the School of Music at Howard, directed the chapel choir for which I had been selected. Dr. Lawson also led our twenty-five-member *a cappella* choir that toured over spring break every year. We stayed in private homes and often sang at other black universities around the country.

I still recall one of Dr. Lawson's vocal exercises. He instructed us to listen closely to the person singing next to us, reminding us that singing in a choir is not like singing a solo. Then he said something profound. If you want to make a beautiful sound, you should always try to match the voice of the person next to you.

Looking back, I realize that Dr. Lawson was teaching more than a musical technique. It was a message about life. When we really listen to each other, we are better able to build community.

———•◦•———

It seems in life that there are moments when a person says something unexpected that sticks to the walls of your mind. Louise Latham, the assistant dean of women and resident counselor of Sojourner Truth Hall at Howard University, made such a statement. Perhaps the rhyming words make it memorable, but the message about humility was powerful and has persisted. She said, "It's not by your roots nor by your toots but by your fruits that you shall be known."

The chair of Howard's department of sociology, Dr. E. Franklin Frazier, was well respected for his studies of black culture, including the social classes within the black community. I was particularly interested in his work on the integral part religion played in shaping the lives of black people. Though Dr. Frazier usually lectured and invited little student interaction, one day he asked us to share our religious backgrounds. It became apparent that I was the only person in the class who had been raised in the Church of God tradition. Most students were Baptist, Methodist, or Episcopal. I felt uncomfortable when other students began to quiz me: Are you a Holy Roller? Do you speak in tongues? They had little understanding of the Church of God tradition.

———•◦•———

Dr. Frank Snowden always carried a special green bag, a tell-tale sign that he had studied at Harvard as an undergraduate. At Howard he made literature and philosophy come alive teaching in the humanities. Known as a stickler for vocabulary building and understanding the origin of words, Dr. Snowden is memorable to me more because of relationships. I recall the way in which he so lovingly talked about his wife and his daughter, sharing stories about their travels to Europe and beyond. Though he probably didn't realize it at the time, he gave me a glimpse into what kind of marriage and family life I wanted to have one day.

Many of the Howard students did not share my Christian upbringing. Even Mamie, my freshman roommate, showed little interest in matters of faith or attending chapel. One night, however, she overhead me praying about a challenging exam I was facing. Later when Mamie and I were hoping to pledge Alpha Kappa Alpha sorority, she said, "Maybe you should say a prayer for us." I couldn't help but think that a tiny seed had been planted.

MEETING LARRY

During my time at Howard University, I noticed a handsome male student dressed in a camel coat and yellow tie, brown trousers and argyle socks. We had previously been seated next to each other for a lecture; but on this particular day, my interest was piqued as we passed each other on the staircase. His name was Lawrence "Larry" Roberts.

A short time later, the university sponsored a Sadie Hawkins dance in which young women were encouraged to ask male students to be their dates for the evening. I chose to go alone rather than ask Larry or another student. When I arrived at the dance, I spied Larry standing in the long line to check coats. I boldly asked if I could check my coat with his. He said yes and we had a brief conversation. Even though I kept my eyes peeled through the evening, I didn't see him again until the dance was over.

Not long after, I looked out the dorm window to see Larry coming up the long walk toward the front door. I listened for my buzzer, hoping it would go off to tell me that I had a guest. It did not sound, but I could hear the buzzer in another girl's room. A few minutes later I looked out the window to see him walking out with one of my classmates. I definitely felt disappointed. However, when the new semester began, it turned out that Larry and I had a physical science class together. Soon we became friends; and the rest, as they say, is history.

Larry was drafted to serve in World War II, but after he returned and I had graduated from Howard, we married in my parents' backyard. On the day of the wedding, we dismissed the notion that a groom should not see the bride until she's coming down the aisle. We realized that if we wanted much of a wedding, we had work to do! Together, Larry and

I set up white chairs and a trellis that we'd borrowed from the church. We tied crepe paper bows on the branches of the apple tree, making it appear to be in full bloom. It was a joyous day, the first of a fifty-seven-year marriage.

———•·•———

It seems that throughout my life, there have always been people around to remind me of the value of integrity, character, and love. Even on those occasions when I felt intimidated by my peers or my circumstances, I somehow knew that God would direct my way if I would just listen.

HEBREWS 13:6-8

So we say with confidence,
"The Lord is my helper; I will not be afraid.
What can mere mortals do to me?"
Remember your leaders, who spoke the word
of God to you.
Consider the outcome of their way of life
and imitate their faith.
Jesus Christ is the same yesterday
and today and forever.

Robin's *Reflection*

People often ask me what is the secret to my success. I tell them, being the daughter of Lawrence and Lucimarian Roberts. They made me believe anything was possible. It had to be terrifying for Mom to leave her family in Akron, Ohio, and go to college in Washington, DC, but she did it.

My parents fell in love at Howard. I know they hoped one of their four children would attend their alma mater, but we all chose other colleges. For Butch it was Rutgers; Sally-Ann went to the University of Southern Mississippi; Dorothy attended William Carey College; and I went to Southeastern Louisiana University. Fortunately, my niece, Judith, saved the day. She graduated from Howard's School of Medicine in 2010, our family's first doctor and a Howard grad!

Like my mom, at times I've been scared to venture outside my comfort zone. But every day I say the Prayer for Protection she taught me the first time I moved away from home:

> The light of God surrounds me;
> The love of God enfolds me;
> The power of God protects me;
> The presence of God watches over me;
> Wherever I am, God is!*

*Prayer for Protection, James Freeman, 1941

Chapter **6**

STANDING ON HOLY GROUND

Over the years I have learned that wherever we stand is holy ground if God is revealed and revered there. Holy moments from my earliest days are forever imprinted on my heart.

Each summer when I was growing up, I rediscovered a bit of heaven on earth. It could be found at the West Middlesex Campground in southwestern Pennsylvania, a place where Church of God members from around the region would gather on the first Sunday in August for a ten-day spiritual retreat. I looked forward to campground all year long. It was an idyllic getaway for rest and renewal for people of all ages.

Usually I squeezed in between my two aunts in the backseat of my grandparents' Whippet roadster to make the trip from Akron to West Middlesex. They always went a few days early to set up their concession booths. Though my grandfather owned the car, he had never learned to drive; so my Uncle George would take the steering wheel under my grandfather's watchful eye. My mother stayed behind in Akron to work but always managed to get to campground with my brother and sister for a few days later in the week.

Although we drove only sixty miles from our home to reach campground, it might as well have been on the other side of the world. The trip seemed to take forever as we bumped over the hilly terrain until at last campground opened up into full view. Spread out in a clearing lay a scattering of humble cottages, a motel-like lodge, and a large community dining room. But the wooden tabernacle stood as the centerpiece. It served as the gathering place where people would come all through the day for music, seminars, and worship.

In many ways, campground was like a huge family reunion where we connected with people of our denomination from places as far away as Chicago and New York. Some of the participants had purchased a modest cottage of their own. The cottages were nothing fancy and primarily were used for sleeping since none included kitchens. Everyone ate in the large community-dining hall, which gave us an opportunity to meet new people. Most families rented rooms at the lodge or rented one of the cottages. Year after year, I was overwhelmed by the sense of community borne out in the lives of these people who sacrificed time and money to come together to worship and to encourage one another.

One of the men walked through the campground swinging a large bell to announce each prayer and worship service. I would slide onto the tabernacle's rough-hewn benches and listen to passionate sermons by the guest preachers. But it was when we lifted our voices together in song that I knew exactly why I was drawn to this sacred place. This was holy ground.

When I was twelve, the director of the music program invited me to be a member of the mass choir. I was thrilled by his invitation since it would make me the youngest member ever to sing with the campground choir. Adding to my excitement, the choir was scheduled to sing at a rally for a U.S. presidential candidate. The radio broadcast of our performance brought a wave of national attention.

In the summers that followed, I was sometimes asked to sing solos and in ensembles. Often I would stay after the evening service to rehearse. In fact, my favorite campground memory is of locking arms with my mother and walking back to my grandparents' cottage following a late-night music rehearsal. My mother would sit patiently on a back row until the rehearsal ended so that she could accompany me safely home in the inky blackness of night.

As teenagers, a group of us hiked through the hills around campground one warm afternoon. We stumbled upon a spring of cool water nestled beside a lush meadow. A weathered woodshed stood guard over the spring. After a long hike, we eagerly scooped up the water and savored the cool wetness.

The following year, my friends and I returned to the spring that we had come to regard as our special place. This time we discovered that the shed had been boarded up. Painted across it was a word of caution: *Contaminated!* There was lively conversation among our group before my adventurous friend Patty Heard and two others decided to disregard the warning. I remember being quite anxious, trying to dissuade them from drinking the spring water. They drank it anyway, saying that it looked perfectly fine to them.

Over the course of a few weeks, the three who had gulped the water became seriously ill. Each was diagnosed with typhoid fever. Not long after, my friend Patty died. After a long hospitalization, the other two finally recovered.

It was a sorrowful time. Of course, Patty's parents were heartbroken by the loss of their only daughter. Years later, when Larry and I were planning our wedding, my mother suggested that we ask Patty's father, a minister, to officiate at the ceremony. On the day of the wedding, Rev. Heard struggled through the marriage liturgy. His voice broke and his hands trembled. Undoubtedly his thoughts were on Patty and what might have been for her life.

Once I started college, I could no longer attend campground since I needed to work to save as much money as I could. But years later, Larry and I had the opportunity to share the campground experience with all of our children. At the time Larry was stationed in New Jersey. I remember that my mother invited sixteen-year-old Butch to help out with one of the concession booths. He gladly accepted her offer but still laughs about the hard lesson he learned that week. Dipping ice cream for hundreds of people is not as easy as it sounds!

Not long after Robin was born, Larry and I were able to surprise my mother by purchasing one of the little cottages at campground as a gift for her. To pay for it, we had to take out a small loan, but I will never forget the joy that danced in her eyes when we gave her the news. Campground was such an important part of her faith journey—and of mine.

REVIVALS AND RETREATS

Growing up in Akron, I also anticipated the spring revival hosted by my church each year. There was always an out-of-town evangelist whose dynamic preaching style struck a chord with me. One of my favorite evangelists was an entertainer of sorts. I remember watching him create interesting dance steps in the pulpit as we all sang an uplifting hymn. Usually at the conclusion of each service, the evangelist would offer an altar call for those who felt compelled to give their life to Christ. As a young girl, the pull to walk forward was strong even though I didn't yet feel prepared to offer my life in total commitment. So time and time again, as the congregation sang "Softly and Tenderly Jesus Is Calling," I would step out into the aisle, kneel at the front of the church, and whisper to the minister, "Just pray for me. Please, just pray for me."

My young heart was also moved by a foot-washing and Communion service that our church celebrated each year just before Easter. The annual service was intended to reflect Jesus' washing the feet of the disciples and sharing the Last Supper in the upper room. The humbling imagery of this sacred worship service spoke to me: men stooping down to wash the feet of other men on one side of the church; women washing the feet of women on the other side. Towels wrapped around their waists. Basins of water. Even with my head bowed, I couldn't resist a peek at the bare feet of church members waiting for their feet to be washed. In my recollection, I cherish these holy moments.

———·•·———

Years later, Larry and I took our children to a spiritual retreat at Lake George in the Adirondack Mountains of upstate New York. Hosted by the Protestant chapel organization from area military bases, the retreat brought military families together in a spiritual setting. Each family was asked to share devotional time before breakfast every day; the children were to read scripture passages and meditations. We were instructed not to talk to anyone except our own family members during that worship time.

There was something wonderfully tender about gathering as a family unit to worship together in such an exquisite setting. During the day the kids went to workshops, and parents attended seminars. Then at night we all gathered around a campfire after a brief worship service. I sang in the choir and recall being introduced to two wonderful songs: "Kum Ba Yah" and "How Great Thou Art."

On the morning we were to depart, we scurried around packing suitcases and loading the car; then we realized that four-year-old Robin was missing. Suddenly I was thrust into every parent's nightmare. I remember whispering a desperate prayer for her safety.

Larry and I and the older children spread out over the grounds and began calling Robin's name, trying to remain calm as we frantically searched for her. It seemed an eternity before Larry found her sitting at the far end of the pier that stretched out into the cold, deep water of Lake George. She was sitting dangerously at the edge, dangling her legs, swinging them back and forth like a pendulum clock. No doubt she was swept up in her own imagination. Even though we had told her not to go to the lake unless her father or I were present, it seemed the warning had been wasted on a curious preschooler. I can still envision Larry, carefully approaching her, not wanting to startle her and cause her to lose her balance. What sweet relief when he had her safely engulfed in his strong arms.

HOLY MOMENTS ON BASE

Just a short time after our Lake George experience, Larry received an assignment to NATO headquarters in Izmir,

Turkey. Our family traveled in a caravan of buses with others from the base to attend an Easter sunrise service in Ephesus. A trail of red taillights wound through the darkness as we all quietly anticipated the Resurrection story. We arrived just as the sun crept above the horizon in the city where the apostle Paul once stood. As the mass choir sang, "He arose, he arose," I knew my feet were planted on holy ground.

I often reflect back on all the different places where I have had the opportunity to worship as a part of a larger community of believers. For the twenty-five years that our family moved from base to base around the world, the military's chapel program provided a spiritual foundation and sense of continuity. The chapel had a way of bringing strangers together as kindred spirits though we came from different religious and denominational backgrounds. Even the chaplains represented various denominational affiliations, but always an ecumenical spirit bound us together in Christian love.

One time the chapel's Protestant and Catholic women's groups joined together to travel from Izmir to Istanbul, Turkey, for a spiritual pilgrimage to religious sites. The two groups were mostly strangers to one another as we climbed onto a rickety old bus. When the bus came to a high hill, it began to sputter until it could go no further. All of us had to get off and help push the bus up the steep incline. We laughed and fellowshiped while straining to put our force behind the old bus. At that moment, I thought to myself that God was in our midst, bringing us together as pilgrims on the journey of life. Once again, it was holy ground.

Each base's chapel program offered opportunities for service and participation. Somehow whenever we would arrive at a new base, word would get out that I could play the piano. Although I had never been trained as an organist, many times I found myself playing the organ for chapel worship services. I quickly learned that each chaplain had a different worship style, so I had to adjust to each preference. One of the chaplains came from a Baptist background and asked to have soft organ music play in the background as he was concluding his prayer. On one particular Sunday, the organ pedal got stuck, so that when I began to play, the music was exceedingly loud. No doubt, the sound startled everyone, including the chaplain. I struggled to get the volume turned down, but the chaplain finally gave up and roared a final amen.

While stationed at Keesler Air Force Base in Biloxi, a young black chaplain requested permission to offer a Soul Service that would meet the needs of men and women who were not comfortable with a formal worship service. I will never forget the first Soul Service. The choir started at the back of the chapel and came down the aisle, swaying in unison as they sang "Marching to Zion." A palpable energy and passion filled the room. It was holy ground, indeed. I was so moved by the experience that I told my family I was thinking of joining the choir. That's when Dorothy burst into laughter and said I would have trouble singing while swaying at the right time and in the right direction.

Another time on a different base, I remember how my heart was tendered to look out from the choir loft and see Butch ushering alongside his dad on a special father-son Sunday. Knowing that Larry was modeling his Christian faith for his son, it was another moment in which I sensed God's holy presence.

In Hard Times

That same sense of holiness swept over me again at Larry's memorial service in 2004. Though I was deeply grieving my loss, I strongly felt God's presence in the chapel at Keesler Air Force Base in Biloxi. Speakers filled the service with eloquent words about Larry and his lifetime of achievements as a Tuskegee Airman and a retired U.S. Air Force colonel. As we processed behind the casket, we began to sing, "When We All Get to Heaven." My children say that I lifted my arms and began to direct everyone to sing as I walked up the aisle since it appeared that our Jewish friend and organist was not familiar with the song. Soon everyone was singing, and I was moved.

I felt the deep presence of God as we joyously reaffirmed our belief that we would all be together again one day. Later, I was touched to hear Robin's *Good Morning America* colleague Charles Gibson comment that he had never been to a more uplifting celebration of life.

———◆———

Less than a year after Larry died, Hurricane Katrina ravaged the Gulf Coast. I was holed up in my Biloxi home with three other family members, silently questioning my decision not to evacuate and beginning to wonder if we would live or die. As wind ripped off portions of the roof, Katrina plunged me into the arms of God. Yes, we were exposed and vulnerable, but there was comfort and hope in the promises of God as we sang and prayed. The rain-soaked carpet beneath my feet was indeed holy, for God was in our midst.

Just two years later, I stood with my daughters Sally-Ann and Dorothy at the bedside of my youngest daughter, Robin, who was about to undergo surgery for a cancerous tumor in her breast. My thoughts flashed back to the young girl who had sat so dangerously close to the edge of the pier, swinging her legs. No matter how old our children are, parents want to keep them safe and healthy. A mother's prayer formed on my lips. *God, please protect my child.* I opened my eyes to look down and see the feet of Robin's sisters surrounding her hospital bed. It was another bit of holy ground.

———◆———

Every time our family gathered for a holiday celebration and we sang hymns, held hands, and prayed together, God was among us. Today when I look into the faces of four generations of family members and give thanks, I am reminded that even my own living room is holy ground.

Marching to Zion

Come, we that love the Lord,
and let our joys be known;
join in a song with sweet accord,
join in a song with sweet accord
and thus surround the throne, and thus surround the throne.

We're marching to Zion, beautiful, beautiful Zion;
we're marching upward to Zion, the beautiful city of God.

Then let our songs abound,
and every tear be dry;
we're marching through Emmanuel's ground,
we're marching through Emmanuel's ground,
to fairer worlds on high, to fairer worlds on high.

We're marching to Zion, beautiful, beautiful Zion;
we're marching upward to Zion, the beautiful city of God.

LAMENTATIONS 3:22-24

Because of the LORD's great love
we are not consumed,
for his compassions never fail.
They are new every morning;
great is your faithfulness.
I say to myself, "The LORD is my portion;
therfore I will wait for him."

Robin's *Reflection*

Nothing—and I mean nothing—makes Mom happier than hearing people say that they saw one of her children in church. She enjoys telling a story about me when I was seven years old and we were living in Izmir, Turkey.

Every Sunday as a family we would head into the city for church. One Sunday I saw a homeless man with no legs outside the church. I was clutching a coin in my hand to put in the offering. Instead, I handed it to this man. You would have thought I had given him a million dollars by his reaction of joy and gratitude.

Every Sunday from then on I couldn't wait to jump out of the car, race up to the man, and give him my coin. He was always there waiting for me. It's a powerful memory. At that young age my mom had already taught me it is better to give than to receive.

Chapter 7

OPENING DOORS OF OPPORTUNITY

Sitting next to Eleanor Roosevelt at an elegant dinner seemed like a dream. Who could have imagined that Lucimarian Tolliver, daughter of a domestic worker and an alcoholic father, would be a foot away from the former First Lady of the United States? I was a senior at Howard University and could barely wrap my mind around the reality.

A few years before this luncheon, Mrs. Roosevelt had made newspaper headlines when she abruptly resigned from the Daughters of the American Revolution to protest the DAR's refusal to rent its Constitution Hall for a concert given by black opera singer Marian Anderson. Now I was seated next to her, the First Lady who had done so much to publicly confront the injustices of racism and segregation.

Dr. Mordecai Johnson, president of Howard University, often invited dignitaries to the campus as a way to introduce students to prominent individuals involved in humanitarian causes. I was one of only two seniors invited for this occasion. As the president of Howard University Women's League, I was asked to sit on one side of Mrs. Roosevelt. A male student representing the young men of Howard sat on her other side. I remember being impressed by how articulate Mrs. Roosevelt was, asking questions and then listening attentively to my answers. But only in retrospect do I realize just how blessed I was to have had that opportunity.

COLLEGIATE OPPORTUNITIES

My years at Howard University overflowed with other opportunities I had never expected. Besides the honor of sitting next to the First Lady and being selected president of Women's League, I was the president of my dormitory, Frazier Hall, during my junior year. For my senior year, I was elected by my classmates to be one of the mentors at Sojourner Truth Hall, the residence hall for freshmen women. It was a special honor because students were asked to select a senior classmate they would most want to mentor their younger sisters. I also took great pride in participating in my sorority, Alpha Kappa Alpha, which was founded at Howard in 1908. And of course, I was active in the chapel choir program.

I confess that a certain amount of esteem came with these leadership positions. But if ever I began to feel too puffed up and proud, the words of my wise mother came circling back through my mind. It was a simple but weighty warning: "When you strut, you stumble."

During my junior year, I was especially pleased that my mother was able to attend a mother-daughter tea hosted by the university. She preferred to travel by bus and had saved enough money for a ticket for a long weekend in Washington. A fashion-conscious friend from Akron advised her in selecting clothes suitable for the occasion. I met my mother at the bus station, then took her on a tour of the campus where she met some of my classmates and their mothers. As evening came, my roommate and I gave our dorm room to our mothers while we bunked in another room with fellow students. In truth, we should not be credited for our gracious hospitality. We just didn't want to share a room with our mothers, who snored!

On the day of the tea, my eyes rimmed with tears of joy. My mother felt so proud to be included in this special event. I remember glancing at her work-worn hands and thinking of all the things she had sacrificed to help get me to this place in time.

When I graduated from Howard University in 1946, jobs were not easy to find, even for college graduates—and definitely for black graduates. I had decided that I would take a job at Goodyear Aircraft in Akron when I couldn't find a job in my career field. But at my father's suggestion, I returned home and began to volunteer as a social worker in the juvenile court system. He had been concerned that by accepting a factory job, I would send a negative signal to other young black women that college had not been worth the effort. Thankfully my volunteer work as a caseworker was gratifying and soon led to a paid position at the Akron Children's Home where I continued to hone my skills. After Larry and I married in 1947, I was able to use my teaching skills in various locations, including Japan and Turkey. Even my experience as a mother of four children and an officer's wife helped prepare me for future opportunities.

OPPORTUNITIES TO GIVE AND SERVE

Though I never made my goal to be the first woman of anything, I can't help but smile a bit when I look back and see how doors opened up to me, even as a middle-aged and older woman. I was the first black woman to become president of the seven-hundred-member Keesler Officers' Wives Club and was selected Keesler's Military Wife of the Year. I was the first woman to serve as president of the Mississippi Coast Coliseum Commission, first woman to chair the Mississippi State Board of Education, and first woman to serve on the board of directors of the Mississippi Power Company. I also chaired the New Orleans Branch of the Federal Reserve Bank of Atlanta and served on the advisory board for the Boys and Girls Club of the Mississippi Gulf Coast. Then at age eighty-seven, I learned that I had been awarded the Mississippi

Medal of Service for contributions made to improve local communities and the state.

It seemed that each opportunity came from somewhere out of the blue. And with every new task came another occasion to meet new people and learn things that would help me along the way.

———•———

When Larry and I settled in Pass Christian, it was the first time we were able to look for a permanent church home. Robin was in high school and the other children either in college or grown. We found our church home at First Presbyterian Church of Bay Saint Louis where we met Rev. Dwyn Mounger. The church has since been renamed Old Town Presbyterian Church and is just across the bridge from Pass Christian. Rev. Mounger became a good friend and guided both Larry and me toward local, regional, and national church leadership positions for the Presbyterian Church (USA).

After browsing booths for various agencies and ministries at a PCUSA General Assembly in 1985, I found myself drawn to the national board for Presbyterian Church's Self-Development of People (SDOP), led by Dr. Frederic Walls at that time. The ministry aims to help people around the world help themselves. Instead of just giving money to the impoverished or oppressed, the SDOP partners with groups who have identified their needs and have developed a plan to change their situation, preserving their dignity and self-respect. If approved by the SDOP national committee, the group then receives a grant from the PCUSA.

Though in my seventies at the time, the idea of being a part of something much bigger than myself excited me, and I soon became an SDOP board member. Dr. Walls set a clear vision for mission; and Cynthia White, then associate, now director for SDOP, helped me understand the collaborative efforts between the church and those who desperately needed resources. With the board's support, I traveled to places like Guatemala, Puerto Rico, and Egypt to do site visits and witnessed firsthand how lives were being changed because of the church's participation.

Late one night during my tenure on the SDOP board, an eye-opening experience at the local grocery store made me think about ministry and mission in a new way. Larry waited for me in the car while I went inside the store to pick up a gallon of milk. As I walked to the back of the nearly empty store, a man who looked as if he had been dusted in flour startled me. He asked me for money. I instinctively replied that I had no cash and scurried away.

At the checkout counter, I chose to use a check instead of cash because I was afraid he might be watching and would know I had lied to him. I returned to the car and asked Larry if he had seen the strange man leave the store. Larry insisted that I was the only person who had come out the door.

Later, my reaction to this man haunted me. Had I been peering into the eyes of Christ? Why hadn't I offered to buy him food? I have often thought that God was reminding me not to make snap judgments about people, even when the situation is uncomfortable. Another lesson learned.

───•◦•───

Throughout my life, it seems that when I have been obedient to God, doors have opened. Although I wasn't always aware of it at the time, the hardships of life have better prepared me for the next leg of the journey. Only when I look back across the landscape of my life do I see how each stone on the pathway led me from poverty to possibility.

Leaning on the Everlasting Arms

What a fellowship, what a joy divine,
leaning on the everlasting arms;
what a blessedness, what a peace is mine,
leaning on the everlasting arms.
Leaning, leaning, safe and secure from all alarms;
leaning, leaning, leaning on the everlasting arms.

JEREMIAH 7:23
I gave them this command: Obey me,
and I will be your God and you will be my people.

Robin's *Reflection*

Whenever I'm waiting for Mom in the airport baggage claim area, people from her flight let me know she's on her way. I always wonder, *How do all these people know she's my mom?* It's because she has never met a stranger. She talks to everyone. Mom enjoys visiting me in New York City and having lunch at a sidewalk cafe. She gets a kick out of looking at people up and down as they pass by our table. I'll say: "Mom, stop staring!" She responds: "I'm not staring, honey, I'm people watching." Mom has a wonderful sense of humor.

One day, some years ago, I was riding in the car with her at the wheel when she accidentally cut off another driver. At the next light the driver pulled up next to Mom's car and was telling her off. I had the urge to jump out and give this guy a piece of my mind. But before I could, Mom calmly rolled down her window and sweetly said to him, "Your Momma." I don't know who was more stunned, him or me!

Chapter **8**

Growing older, celebrating life

A few years ago I was homeless. At least that's how I felt. It seemed that at my late age, I had no particular place to go, no place to call home. Hurricane Katrina had turned my world upside down. My home in Pass Christian was uninhabitable, and I wasn't sure if I should sell it as-is or refurbish and renovate it. My second home in Biloxi had withstood the hurricane but suffered severe damage from water and wind. Then just a few months after Katrina had made her unwelcome arrival, I had a dreadful bout with pneumonia. For a while I lived in a rehabilitation center, wondering where I would go when I was released.

Recalling that stressful season of life, I realize I was still numb from everything that had happened in recent years. Within a short period of time, my life had unraveled through a series of tragic events that began when my son-in-law Willie Craft, Sally-Ann's husband, was diagnosed with colon cancer and died just six months later. The next year, my husband, Larry, suffered a heart attack and unexpectedly passed away in his sleep. Soon after that, I was diagnosed with a neurological disorder and a degenerative bone disease that had my daughter Dorothy ushering me to countless doctors' offices and hospitals. In August of 2005, Hurricane Katrina blew through the Gulf Coast. Then in 2007, Robin received the devastating news that she had an aggressive form of breast cancer.

I lived in a hazy fog during much of that period of time, waffling back and forth on almost every decision. Seeing that I was weary and worn, my grown children took charge of my life as best they could. I think we were all wondering if I should just pull up stakes and move from the Gulf Coast. But where would I go? I had already tried a couple of senior living options, including an assisted living center near Robin; but nothing seemed quite right. I kept asking myself what I was supposed to be doing at this stage of life. In all honesty, I felt frazzled and totally useless.

Even in those dark days, my faith served as my source of comfort. Today, I happily live back in my Pass Christian home where I play my piano and sing hymns every day. A home health-care aide comes here to assist me several times during the week. Physically, I have good days and bad. At times my joints are stiff and my words are slow, but I remind myself of an important truth: God has given me purpose that overcomes pain.

———•—•———

One of the best things about growing old is being able to look back and see God's hand at work through the years. I have truly enjoyed watching my grandfather's spiritual seeds grow into something he probably never could have imagined. Before I was born, he had started a Sunday school class in the living room of his Akron home. As the group grew in size, members determined to convert a nearby dance hall into the Roberts Street Church of God that I attended as a child.

Today the church has relocated to a larger facility and has been renamed as Arlington Church of God in Akron. It houses a senior center, a K–8 academy, a community center, and a preschool program funded by the estate of a longtime organist for the church.

No longer is it the little neighborhood church where I played "King, off my mountain" with my friends on the concrete block wall after Sunday school. But even as it has grown, the church remembers its rich history. My grandfather's photograph still hangs on the church wall, honoring him as the founding pastor. My Uncle George, who had driven my grandparents' car to campground, also became a minister and carried on the faith traditions he learned from his parents. There's no doubt that my grandfather would be humbled to know that all of these blessings came from the tiny seeds that he planted years ago.

Regrettably, my grandfather died when I was a junior in college, so he never got to know my father as a sober man. My father first sought help for his alcoholism through a program at Johns Hopkins University Hospital. But it was not until I was married and had a child that he joined an Alcoholics Anonymous group in Akron and finally succeeded in maintaining his sobriety.

My father was the only black man in his AA group. Many of the other members had been his drinking buddies, including a number of Irish immigrants. Together they went through the Twelve Step program, forming a strong bond over the years. My father soon recognized a need for an AA group for black men who would be intimidated in an all-white setting. He received permission from a Catholic church with a large African-American membership to start the first black AA group in Akron in their building.

As my father continued his sobriety, he began to speak to groups around the region. One of the AA founders heard him and was so impressed with my father's compassionate leadership and his progress in dealing with his own addiction that he helped my father obtain the capital he needed to open a Pure Oil service station in Akron. Gradually, life for my parents began to improve. My father's business became successful enough so that my mother could finally retire from her housekeeping jobs.

Today I am grateful that my children knew their grandfather only as a sober man who was warm and witty. And though my father had never been a church person, he became a student of the Bible and spent his time ministering to alcoholics at the county jail and the Salvation Army. I'd like to think my grandfather would have approved.

REMEMBERING MY TRAVELS

As I continue to age, I find great pleasure in recalling the interesting places I've traveled to in my lifetime. Mostly because of Larry's military service, I have experienced cultures I had only read about in books. From Japan to Egypt, Hong Kong to Paris, I have been blessed with memories of faraway places, memories that soothe me as I grow older. And the greatest joy was to have shared some of those experiences with my children.

When Larry was assigned to Izmir, Turkey, our family seized the chance to immerse ourselves in a culture much different from our own. We had decided to look for housing in the Turkish community instead of within an enclave of Americans. Admittedly, leaving Butch back at Rutgers University in New Jersey was painful; but the girls were excited about this international adventure, and Butch would have the opportunity to visit over summer break.

Larry, the girls, and I rode the trolley into Izmir, then walked around town, scouring apartment buildings and searching for windows with no draperies, an indication that the apartment was vacant. Finally we discovered a delightful apartment with marble floors on a little inlet of the Aegean Sea. It became our base for exploring the history and traditions of Turkey. We made friends with the Turkish people in our neighborhood, shopped in the local markets, ate Turkish food, and tried to learn their language.

Not long after our family arrived, we heard a knock at our door. A Turkish husband and wife had discovered that I was an American with a college degree and teaching experience. In Turkey, the schools were run by business professionals, and they wanted to know if I would teach English to their students. Larry was surprised at my enthusiasm, but I jumped at the chance, even though it required my taking two buses to reach the school. Over the months that followed, I grew close to the students and learned much about their Muslim faith. When we left Turkey to return to the U.S., the students gave me a beautiful black lacquered plaque decorated with an image of a mosque. On the back, the students had signed their names. I treasured that gift. Sadly, it was lost when Hurricane Katrina ravaged my Pass Christian home. Still, the memories that our family made while living in Turkey remain and bring me great joy in this season of life.

In 2004 Larry and I took a trip-of-a-lifetime to South Africa along with other family members. Larry had dreamed of this trip for years and had his camera poised to capture every memorable sight. In Kruger National Park, we awoke each day to playful monkeys swinging in the trees nestled close to our window. We rode in an open-air vehicle across the expanse of unspoiled landscape, staying alert to magnificent wildlife at every turn. It was winter there; and by the time we started back to the lodge, it was growing dark. A guide sitting on the hood of the van held a large spotlight to illuminate the way. As we approached the lodge, my breath was suddenly taken away at the sight of torches flickering in the darkness and lining the pathways around the lodge. It was one of those unforgettable, pinch-me moments in life.

Another of those moments came just days later when we toured Nelson Mandela's home in Soweto and his prison cell on Robben Island. I was overcome with a wave of emotion, standing at the cell bars of the prison. Just thinking about the power of one man's courage and forgiveness in the face of injustice was almost more than I could bear.

Little did we know that the South Africa journey would be the last trip Larry would take before he died. Once we returned to Mississippi, he spent days preparing a slide-show program of our trip that he presented to the local Rotary Club. On the morning he died, he was scheduled to help Dorothy present a similar program for the local library. In the days after his memorial service, I kept thinking about how grateful I was that we'd had the opportunity to fulfill his dream and celebrate life together in South Africa.

HONORING LARRY'S LIFE

After fifty-seven years of marriage, I found it hard to be alone. Even though I was accustomed to Larry being away on military assignments, we had always been tethered to each other, to our family, and to God. My personal sadness was magnified by the fact that Larry passed away before the Tuskegee Airmen were awarded the Congressional Medal of Honor in 2007. He had been part of this pioneering group of courageous black men who displayed amazing courage, patriotism, and flying skill. Many say their success put the armed forces on the track to desegregate.

On the day when President George W. Bush awarded the medals in Washington, DC, I noticed many of the men depended on walkers or wheelchairs for mobility. Others, like Larry, had died before receiving the prestigious tribute. How I wish these brave men could have been honored when they were younger. Still, I was proud that Larry had been one of the Tuskegee Airmen and was thrilled to learn that Keesler Air Force Base planned to dedicate a building to him.

The dedication ceremony for the new Consolidated Aircraft Maintenance Facility to honor Colonel (Ret.) Lawrence E. Roberts was scheduled for August 28, 2009. Because of health issues, I could not attend the dedication, but Major General Alfred Flowers arranged for me to watch it live on the computer. I was so thankful that three of our children were able to attend. Robin was on an assignment. Butch,

Sally-Ann, and Dorothy each spoke eloquently about their father. Dorothy read a letter that I had written for the occasion. Since that time, the Keesler Air Force Base chapter of the Tuskegee Airmen was also named in Larry's honor. Now it all seems a fitting remembrance of Lawrence E. Roberts who had started and ended his military career at Keesler.

War Memorial Park in Pass Christian also honors Larry's life through a tree sculpture created by Florida artist Marlin Miller. Following Hurricane Katrina, Miller donated his time and talent to carve works of art from the trunks of dead oak trees all along the Mississippi Gulf Coast highway. Dedicated to Larry's memory, the magnificent carved eagle is poised as though ready to take flight. I take great comfort in knowing the beautiful sculpture will be standing for years to come.

As I sat in War Memorial Park during the dedication ceremony, I realized that I had been harboring resentment about the way Larry had been slighted at the end of his military career. After thirty years of service and many medals and awards, he did not receive the traditional tributes that others of the same rank received at their retirement. For Larry there was no announcement or formal dinner. No dignitaries or special reviewing of the troops. Larry never uttered a disparaging word, but my heart had ached for him. Yet as I looked at the eagle woodcarving, I felt that I had to forgive. The words of "Hear Ye the Master's Call" played in my head.

Hear Ye the Master's Call

Wait not for men to laud, heed not their slight;
Winning the smile of God brings its delight!
Aiding the good and true ne'er goes unblest,
All that we think or do, be it the best.

Learning Over a Lifetime

Over the span of my long life, I have learned many lessons. To be honest, I am learning them still. Out of the tragedy of Hurricane Katrina, I discovered not to prize possessions too highly. I grieved the loss of many special objects: the copper wall plaques we'd brought back from Japan; the china vase hand-painted by Larry's aunt; our stereo and collection of old record albums; my organ. Even now, there are times when I suddenly think about an item only to realize it has been lost forever. I have also discovered what it's like to lose a loved one in a heartbeat. But through every loss, I am learning to loosen my grasp on things of this world and to cling to good memories and to God instead.

I have also come to understand that having a sense of humor offsets the challenges of growing old. My spirits are lifted whenever I hear laughter around the dinner table or at a family gathering. In fact, I often think that humor may be God's best gift to those of us in late life, a salve for challenging moments.

As my mother grew older, she sometimes talked about death and what she wanted for her funeral. She dreaded the thought of people looking down at her lifeless body laid out in a casket, then muttering some nonsense about how natural she looked. In her opinion, people never really look natural when they are dead.

When my mother passed away, my sister and I went to the funeral home only to discover that our mother had bright red nails and lipstick. Depholia and I looked at each other and burst out laughing, thinking back to what mother had said. Sally Tolliver had never worn nail polish or lipstick, so we were certain that no one would look at her and say that she looked natural! Sometimes you just have to laugh.

———·•·———

Standing on the far side of life's time line, I admit that there are days when I feel like a stranger in this world. There are moments when I grumble about being out-of-step with popular culture. I grieve when I see people willing to swap integrity for popularity or financial gain.

When I visit my hometown of Akron, I am reminded of how much life has changed. Many of the things of my childhood are gone. In reality, change is natural. Life goes on. Loved ones die or move away. Expressways stand where familiar buildings used to be. The neighborhood where my story began is not the place of its ending. Nothing stays the same except my steadfast God.

For years I have read and reread the devotions from one of my mother's favorite books, *Streams in the Desert*. Recently the words to one of the devotions reminded me of how aging is preparing me to leave my earthly tent as I anticipate an eternal home with God.

> The owner of the house I have lived in for many years has notified me that he will do little or nothing to keep it in repair. He also advised me to be ready to move.
>
> At first this was not very welcome news. In many respects the surrounding area is quite pleasant, and if not for the evidence of a somewhat declining condition, the house seems rather nice. Yet a closer look reveals that even a light wind causes it to shake and sway, and its foundation is not sufficient to make it secure. Therefore I am getting ready to move.
>
> As I consider the move, it is strange how quickly my interest is transferred to my prospective new home in another country.*

Aging is not something to be dreaded. In spite of its hardships, it is a journey to be embraced. Now that I have grown older, I read the following passage from Dr. Howard Thurman's *Deep Is the Hunger* with a greater understanding.

*L. B. Cowman, comp., *Streams in the Desert: 366 Daily Devotional Readings*, ed. James Reimann (Grand Rapids, MI: Zondervan, 1997), 397 [October 21st Entry].

The fact is, one never comes to the end of anything. Something always remains, some deposit, some residue that mingles with the stream of one's life forever. In a sense, there can never be an end of anything; something remains.*

Thinking about all the stories of my life, one shines notably bright in my memory. My mother loved to tell this story, perhaps because it captured the essence of who I am and what I believe. As I explained earlier, during the Depression my mother cooked on a woodstove in the basement because our electricity had been turned off. On one occasion when my father was home between drinking binges, the family gathered for dinner around a makeshift table in the basement.

For some reason, I began to sing. My father looked at me sternly and announced that there would be no singing at the table. After a few moments, I got up from the table, went outside, and came up to the screened-in window that opened to the basement. I pressed my face close, and I began to sing words that just bubbled up inside me. "I've got a little song in my heart, and I'm going to sing it." I didn't intend to be funny, but even my father could not resist laughing. I suppose I just couldn't be silenced.

---

* Howard Thurman, *Deep Is the Hunger* (New York: Harper, 1951; repr., Richmond, IN: Friends United Press, 1978), 133.

I reflect back on my long life and realize that I still sing because I have a song in my heart and a story to tell about the people who came alongside to encourage me on this journey of life. About a family who has given me bountiful joy and priceless memories. About a God who has been with me each step of the way and will walk with me until I've finished the last mile.

O Love That Wilt Not Let Me Go

O Love that wilt not let me go,
I rest my weary soul in thee;
I give thee back the life I owe,
that in thine ocean depths its flow
may richer, fuller be.

PSALM 100:4B-5
Give thanks to him and praise his name.
For the LORD is good and his love endures forever;
his faithfulness continues through all generations.

Robin's *Reflection*

The stories and wisdom in this chapter are the main reason I prayed Mom would write this book. It can be difficult to watch our parents age. We must remember that it's even more challenging for them. To slowly lose one's independence—being able to drive, to live self-sufficiently. My siblings and I have all asked Mom to live with one of us, but she has refused. She says she doesn't want to be a burden—as if she ever could be that to us. You know what? She still slips me a $20 bill when I come home. She calls it "greasing my palm." She's a proud woman.

Yes, at times the child feels like the parent, but it's so important not to make an aging parent feel like a child. What helps me is knowing that my mom has been—and always will be—a child of God. I love you, Momma.

Letters from Lucimarian's children

Dear Mom,

"Pretty is as pretty does." "If at first you don't succeed, try, try again." "If ifs and ands were pots and pans, there'd be no need for scrubbing." Oh, how I remember your gentle words of encouragement. You made all of your children feel like we were special and there was nothing we couldn't accomplish if we worked and prayed.

There are many things I can thank you and Dad for—food, clothing, shelter, education. But more than anything else, I thank you for sharing your faith. I thank you for living your faith. The love of Jesus was like a sweet aroma in our home wherever we traveled around the world. I treasure memories of you sitting at the piano, playing and singing hymns. "I love to tell the story, 'twill be my theme in glory, to tell the old old story of Jesus and his love." "This is my story, this is my song, praising my Savior all the day long." "Have Thine own way, Lord! Have Thine own way! Thou art the potter; I am the clay." The songs—and there are so many of them—are like a soundtrack in my heart.

I will always remember going to church, Sunday school, and spiritual retreats as a family. God used you and Dad in a mighty way to bless us with God's truth. You didn't preach long sermons. Your life was a sermon. There were the candlelight dinners each night with you and Dad sitting at either end of the table. The food was basic but nourishing: tunafish casserole, hot-dog casserole, fish sticks, fried Spam! Mom, you knew how to stretch those commissary dollars. Yet every meal began with prayer.

Even though you took time to take care of your family, you always found time to be involved in the community. You were concerned about helping others and making your little area of the world better. And you did.

Each day I feel blessed that you are my mother. God bless you, Mom!

Love, Sally-Ann

Dear Mom,

You've taught me many things through the years that I will cherish always. First and foremost, you taught me about universal love. A love that never wavers but grows ever stronger with each and every turn in the road. A love that endures hardship, illness, and any manner of turbulence. A love that grows stronger each day and is, indeed, like our Savior's love, a love that passes all understanding. Even though your speaking at times is difficult, it is not difficult to understand the love behind each word spoken or unspoken. Your love is a precious jewel I try to appreciate each day and share with others as you would have me to do.

This Love is an iron rose whose petals will never die.
Oh, the aroma, the beauty of this wondrous flower
Made from the Spirit of the One Most High
This rose blooms and grows finer each hour.

Your loving son, Butch

Dear Mom,

It's a foggy day here on the Mississippi Gulf Coast as I sit down to write about how you, Lucimarian Tolliver Roberts, have so greatly impacted my life. You've had quite a journey from Lucy Street in Akron, Ohio, to Pass Christian, Mississippi. In these quiet moments I look upon one of my favorite pictures of you and Dad all dressed up at a formal military dinner. The picture captures your youth and vibrancy as you both pose, smiling at the camera. You look like a movie star, and Dad is quite dashing in his white military jacket. You were more than a movie star to me. You were my first teacher!

Your role as my mother involved your earnest desire to teach me right from wrong when I was a child, to know and love God, and to live a faith-filled life as an adult. You have always led by example, and I must admit that I sometimes didn't think I could ever measure up to you. The bar was set high by both you and dad.

Setting the bar high came naturally. Achievement was hoped for and expected of those who are part of the Greatest

Generation. You always wanted the best for your children and made whatever sacrifices were necessary. As a mother now, I'm not sure I could have done what you did for us, especially during the military years.

You had the ability to make every military home we lived in a loving and warm environment. You adorned the oyster white walls with art and family pictures; the linoleum floors were covered with Turkish rugs; and artifacts of military travels filled the coffee table. There were always magazines such as *Ebony* or *Jet* that let us see the accomplishments of others in our race. It was important to you to make sure we knew our world could expand past our home. You wanted us to know we had the ability to soar the world if we so desired.

I haven't quite soared the world, but I owe any successes I have accomplished to you, Mom. I sing because you sing; I laugh because you have taught me to have joy in my heart; and I love because you have given me unconditional love every day of my life! You continue to display tremendous strength through the pains of recent life events, as well as embracing all the blessings God has bestowed on you. You are "still the momma" and a remarkable woman who has certainly left her mark on this world.

I truly am grateful for all you have done for me and my children, Jessica and Lauren, and my grandson, Ryan. I love you now and forever!

Your daughter, Dorothy

Acknowledgments

I am grateful to Missy Buchanan for her gentle understanding of my ups and downs. Her genuine love and concern for those of us who are aging and bewildered by the changes in our lives enable her to capture in printed words the issues we face. She is using her God-given talents of writing and speaking to enlighten and refresh us as we journey home.

Years ago my late friend Violet Dedeaux introduced me to *The Upper Room* daily devotional guide with a gift subscription. Over many years I have been inspired by the pages of stories written by individuals—some jubilant, some poignantly sad but all very real with a message. I am so grateful to Robin Pippin and the Upper Room staff for believing I had a story worthy of a book. I shall forever be grateful to them for allowing me to testify to the glory of God.

I thank the many physicians, nurses, and technicians who patiently listened and heard my litany of aches and pains. Their diagnoses, appropriate medications, or procedures have been invaluable.

My special thanks to Drs. Cyril and Yashashree Bethala, Dr. Andrew Peterson, Dr. Gasque, Dr. Quinos, and Dr. Mark Lachs.

The Commanders of Keesler Air Force Base, their wives and protocol personnel have made every effort to make me feel KAFB will always be my home. Major General Alfred and Ida Flowers, Brigadier General Greg and Charlene Touhill, Colonel and Mrs. Ian Peterson, Colonel Prince and Wanda Guillard.

The Keesler Air Force Base triangle chapel Soul Service. Chaplain Bob and Jackie Jemerson, Chaplain Winston and Kim Jones, Chaplain Ralph and Cherie Elliott and members who have prayed, visited, and flooded me with cards and food. Effie Clarke, Paulette Powell, Val Boswell, Greg Davis, Florence Clay, Chris Moore, Earlie Henson, Gloria Otis.

Pastors and members of First Presbyterian and Old Town Presbyterian Church of Bay St. Louis, Mississippi. Marcia and John Willett, Nora Williams, Janet Galen, Sandra and Billy Power, Lex and Kathy Mauffrey, Virgil and Margaret Harris, Ted and Betty Hanawalt, Al and Carol Shiyou, C. A. and Nancy Russ, and Judy Demarest.

When I was a Girl Scout we sang, "Make new friends but keep the old. One is silver and the other gold." Through the years my silver and gold became intertwined. It is so difficult to discern one from the other. I only know that God has given me many friends who in their own way have demonstrated their love for me—prayer, cards, flowers, food, telephone calls, and visits. So many ways but always just at the time of need. I am blessed to acknowledge in no particular order as each friend is so very dear to me:

Ricky Ingargiola, Cannie Middleton, Mamie Hansberry, Jane Jones Draine, Beverly Cave, Roland and Sharon Weeks, Helen Goodwell, Anne Lott, Dave and Jane Dennis, Ricky and Ann Mathews, Dave and June Vincent, Bill Holmes, Paula April, Diane and John Peranich, Felicia Dunn Burke, Robert and Dara Lee Musso, Bobby Mahoney, Thomas and Claire Rhodeman, Ellie and John Vasilopoulos, Willie and Georgette Cox, Lucy Hazeur, DeAnn Viator, Cynthia and Tommy Mason, Jay and Vickie Trochesset, Anthony and Patsi Topazi, Barbara Salloum, Lee Thomas Barnes, David and Ceceil Ratcliffe, Gerald Piltz, Ellen and John Walsh, Susan L. Taylor, Diane Sawyer, Sherrie and David Westin, Minnie and Jay Venable, Ollie Mae Farmer,Frankie Walton White, Valerie Small, Melva Costen, Alfreida Matthew, Henrietta Drummond, Carter and Penny Bise, Pete and Margaret Carter, Tom and Patsy Spinks, Curtis Kerns, Dick and Jackie Wilson, Helen Mahone and Clifton Walker, the Nabonne, Marshall and Craft families. Governors William (and Elyse) Winter, Ray Maybus, Haley (and Marsha) Barbour.

To my loving family—my many nieces, nephews, and cousins—too many to name, but all have a special place in my heart. My sister, Depholia Sims Butler; although a distance separates us, we are still as close as we were as children. My sisters-in-law, Georgia Roberts and Bessie Tolliver. We three form a solidarity. Our husbands are deceased, but we remember the happy times when our children and husbands shared meals, trips, and other fun times together.

My children who are the loves of my life, Butch and Cynthia, Sally-Ann and Ron, Dorothy, and Robin. Their talents and their love are my joy. My grandchildren, Bianca, Lawrence, Rene, Judith, Jessica, Kelly, Lauren, and Jeremiah. My great grandchildren, Ashley, Jazzlyn, Braylon, Elijah, Ryan, and Kailee round out my circle of love.

Although my hometown is Akron, Ohio, Pass Christian has become my beloved home. Mississippi has embraced me and permitted me to grow spiritually and to be of service.

I know that God will continue to love, guide, and protect us all. And we will be inspired always to know that with God all things are possible. To paraphrase a hymn, there is never a heartache that God does not share. Whether our day is sunny or cloudy, we can know God is always there.

THE STORY BEHIND THIS BOOK

Missy Buchanan

ONE DAY SEVERAL years ago, I answered the telephone and heard a sweet voice ask if I was the author of *Living with Purpose in a Worn-Out Body.* The woman introduced herself as Lucimarian Roberts, and she posed this question: *How did you know what I was thinking when you wrote that book?* Lucimarian said my words had given voice to her thoughts. We talked like old friends that afternoon and subsequently shared more phone conversations and encouraging notes.

When I was invited to tape a segment for *Good Morning America* with Lucimarian and her daughter Robin, coanchor of the show, we finally met in person. I quickly discovered the authentic warmth and humility of both Roberts women.

It has been my privilege to work alongside Lucimarian Roberts on this book. Together we have laughed and shared gumbo and Key lime pie as well as memories. She opened her heart wide to share these stories as she looks back across time to see God's hand in her life.

Upper Room Books is an interdenominational, nonprofit Christian publisher aiming to inspire devotion to God and create Christian community. We are part of Upper Room Ministries, which also publishes *The Upper Room* daily devotional guide, read by more than two million people worldwide and now available as an app for mobile devices.

To learn about our books, visit
www.UpperRoom.org/bookstore